Gambling No More

Self-help, Volume 3

Timothy Scott Phillips

Published by Arcane Horizons Publishing, 2024.

While every precaution has been taken in the preparation of this book, the publisher assumes no responsibility for errors or omissions, or for damages resulting from the use of the information contained herein.

GAMBLING NO MORE

First edition. November 27, 2024.

Copyright © 2024 Timothy Scott Phillips.

ISBN: 979-8230721871

Written by Timothy Scott Phillips.

Table of Contents

To everyone who has felt the weight of gambling addiction—

This book is for you, a reminder that healing and stability are within reach.

To the families and friends who offer unwavering support—

Your love lights the way for recovery.

And to those who have courageously reclaimed their lives from gambling—

Your resilience proves that transformation is possible and hope is never lost.

Introduction

Overview of Compulsive Gambling

COMPULSIVE GAMBLING, also known as gambling addiction or pathological gambling, is a behavioral disorder characterized by an uncontrollable urge to gamble despite the negative consequences it brings. It is a condition that affects millions of people worldwide, transcending age, gender, and socioeconomic status. While gambling can start as a harmless form of entertainment, for some, it escalates into a compulsive behavior that disrupts their lives and the lives of those around them.

Compulsive gambling is classified as an impulse-control disorder, meaning that individuals with this condition find it extremely difficult to resist the urge to gamble, even when they are aware of the detrimental effects. The addiction can take various forms, including casino games, sports betting, online gambling, lottery tickets, and more. What makes gambling particularly insidious is the thrill of the gamble, the euphoria associated with winning, and the false belief that the next big win is just around the corner.

The impact of compulsive gambling is far-reaching. Financial ruin, strained relationships, mental health issues, and even criminal behavior are common consequences. Despite the severity of the problem, many people suffer in silence, feeling ashamed and unable to seek help. This book aims to shed light on the issue of compulsive gambling, offering insights, strategies, and hope to those affected.

Personal Stories and Case Studies

TO UNDERSTAND THE TRUE nature of compulsive gambling, it is essential to hear the stories of those who have lived through it. These personal accounts provide a human face to the statistics and help illustrate the profound impact of the disorder. Here are a few case studies that highlight different aspects of compulsive gambling.

Case Study 1: Jane's Story

JANE, A 45-YEAR-OLD mother of two, began gambling casually with friends at local casinos. Initially, it was a fun way to unwind on weekends. However, as her winnings grew, so did her urge to gamble more frequently. Jane started visiting casinos alone, spending more money than she could afford. Eventually, she began hiding her gambling from her family, using household funds to fuel her addiction. Her behavior became erratic, and she frequently lied about her whereabouts and financial situation. Jane's addiction led to significant debt, causing severe strain on her marriage and family life. After hitting rock bottom, she sought help through a support group and therapy, beginning her journey toward recovery.

Case Study 2: Mark's Story

MARK, A 30-YEAR-OLD software engineer, discovered online sports betting through friends. The convenience and excitement of betting on his favorite sports teams quickly hooked him. What started as small, harmless bets soon spiraled into large, frequent wagers. Mark began skipping work to follow games and place bets, leading to poor job performance and eventually losing his job. His relationships with friends and family deteriorated as he borrowed money and lied to cover his gambling losses. Mark's life became consumed by gambling, leading to severe depression. With the support of his family and professional counseling, Mark is now working towards regaining control of his life.

Case Study 3: Susan's Story

SUSAN, A 60-YEAR-OLD retiree, turned to slot machines at a nearby casino as a way to fill her time and combat loneliness. The flashing lights and sounds of the machines provided a temporary escape from her feelings of isolation. Over time, Susan's gambling escalated, and she began spending her entire pension on slots. She neglected her health and social connections, becoming increasingly isolated and depressed. Realizing the destructive path she was on, Susan sought help from a local support group for seniors with gambling problems. With their encouragement and the help of a therapist, Susan is now rebuilding her life and reconnecting with loved ones.

Goals of the Book

THE PRIMARY GOAL OF this book is to provide a comprehensive guide for individuals struggling with compulsive gambling and those who care about them. Through a blend of personal stories, expert insights, and practical strategies, this book aims to achieve the following objectives:

1. Raise Awareness: Increase understanding of compulsive gambling, its signs, and its impact on individuals and their loved ones. By shedding light on this often-hidden issue, we hope to reduce the stigma and encourage open conversations about gambling addiction.

2. Provide Education: Offer valuable information about the psychological and physiological aspects of compulsive gambling. Understanding the underlying mechanisms of addiction is crucial for both individuals struggling with the disorder and those supporting them.

3. Encourage Self-Reflection: Help readers recognize the signs of compulsive gambling in themselves or others. Through self-assessment tools and personal stories, we aim to foster self-awareness and motivate individuals to seek help.

4. Offer Practical Strategies: Provide actionable steps and strategies for overcoming compulsive gambling. From financial management tips to stress reduction techniques, this book offers a comprehensive toolkit for recovery.

5. Support Recovery: Highlight the importance of building a support system and seeking professional help. By emphasizing the role of therapy, support groups, and family involvement, we aim to create a roadmap for sustained recovery.

6. Inspire Hope: Share success stories of individuals who have overcome compulsive gambling and rebuilt their lives. By showcasing these journeys, we hope to inspire readers and instill a sense of hope that recovery is possible.

7. Promote Long-term Well-being: Focus on maintaining long-term recovery and preventing relapse. This book provides guidance on setting goals, developing healthy habits, and building a fulfilling life free from the grip of gambling addiction.

Moving Forward

AS YOU EMBARK ON THIS journey through the pages of this book, it is important to remember that recovery from compulsive gambling is a process. It requires patience, commitment, and support. Whether you are personally struggling with gambling addiction or supporting someone who is, know that you are not alone. Help is available, and recovery is possible.

This book is your guide to understanding, overcoming, and thriving beyond compulsive gambling. Through education, practical strategies, and inspiring stories, we aim to equip you with the tools you need to reclaim your life and find peace and financial stability.

Let us begin this journey together, one step at a time.

Chapter 1: Understanding Compulsive Gambling

———

Definition and Types of Gambling Addiction

Compulsive gambling, also known as gambling addiction or pathological gambling, is a behavioral disorder characterized by a persistent and uncontrollable urge to gamble, despite the negative consequences it brings. This disorder is recognized by the American Psychiatric Association and is classified as an impulse-control disorder. Individuals with this condition are unable to resist the temptation to gamble, leading to significant disruption in their personal, professional, and financial lives.

Types of Gambling Addiction:

1. ACTION GAMBLING: This type involves gambling for the thrill and excitement. Action gamblers often engage in skill-based games such as poker, sports betting, or blackjack. They are driven by the competitive nature of these activities and the belief that they can outsmart the system or other players.

2. Escape Gambling: Unlike action gamblers, escape gamblers turn to gambling as a way to escape from emotional pain, stress, or life's challenges. They typically engage in chance-based games like slot machines, bingo, or lottery tickets. The repetitive nature of these games provides a temporary distraction from their problems.

3. Binge Gambling: Binge gamblers may not gamble continuously but engage in episodes of intense gambling behavior. These binges can last for days or weeks, during which the individual gambles excessively. After a binge, they might stop for a period, only to relapse again.

4. Online Gambling: With the advent of the internet, online gambling has become increasingly popular. This form of gambling allows individuals to bet on sports, play casino games, or participate in poker tournaments from the

comfort of their homes. The convenience and anonymity of online gambling make it particularly addictive.

Psychological and Physiological Factors

UNDERSTANDING THE PSYCHOLOGICAL and physiological factors that contribute to compulsive gambling is crucial in comprehending the complexity of this disorder. Several factors interplay to drive individuals towards gambling addiction.

Psychological Factors:

1. COGNITIVE DISTORTIONS: Compulsive gamblers often hold irrational beliefs about gambling. These cognitive distortions include the illusion of control, where they believe they can influence the outcome of random events, and the gambler's fallacy, where they think past losses or wins affect future outcomes.

2. Emotional Regulation: Many gamblers use gambling as a way to cope with negative emotions such as anxiety, depression, loneliness, or stress. The excitement of gambling provides temporary relief from these feelings, reinforcing the behavior.

3. Personality Traits: Certain personality traits, such as impulsivity, sensation-seeking, and competitiveness, are associated with a higher risk of developing gambling addiction. These traits can make individuals more prone to engaging in risky behaviors, including gambling.

4. Comorbid Disorders: Compulsive gambling often co-occurs with other mental health disorders, such as depression, anxiety, substance abuse, and personality disorders. These comorbid conditions can exacerbate the severity of gambling addiction and complicate treatment.

Physiological Factors:

1. NEUROTRANSMITTER Imbalances: Research has shown that compulsive gambling is associated with imbalances in certain

neurotransmitters in the brain, such as dopamine and serotonin. Dopamine, in particular, plays a key role in the brain's reward system, and abnormal dopamine activity can lead to compulsive behaviors.

2. Genetic Predisposition: Studies suggest that genetics may play a role in the development of gambling addiction. Individuals with a family history of gambling problems or other addictions are at a higher risk of developing compulsive gambling themselves.

3. Brain Structure and Function: Neuroimaging studies have identified differences in the brain structure and function of compulsive gamblers. These differences are particularly evident in areas of the brain involved in decision-making, impulse control, and reward processing.

How Gambling Affects the Brain

GAMBLING HAS A PROFOUND impact on the brain, particularly in the areas involved in the reward system, decision-making, and impulse control. Understanding these effects can provide insight into why gambling is so addictive and challenging to overcome.

The Reward System:

THE BRAIN'S REWARD system is designed to reinforce behaviors that are essential for survival, such as eating and reproduction, by releasing dopamine, a neurotransmitter associated with pleasure and reward. However, this system can also be hijacked by addictive behaviors, including gambling.

When a person engages in gambling, the anticipation of a potential win triggers the release of dopamine in the brain. This release creates a sense of euphoria and excitement, reinforcing the behavior. Over time, the brain becomes conditioned to associate gambling with pleasure, leading to compulsive behavior.

In compulsive gamblers, the reward system becomes hypersensitive to gambling-related cues. This hypersensitivity results in increased cravings and urges to gamble, even in the face of negative consequences. Additionally, the brain's ability to produce and regulate dopamine becomes impaired, leading to a cycle of addiction where the individual needs to gamble more frequently and with higher stakes to achieve the same level of pleasure.

Decision-Making and Impulse Control:

THE PREFRONTAL CORTEX, a region of the brain responsible for decision-making, impulse control, and executive functions, is significantly affected by gambling. In compulsive gamblers, the prefrontal cortex shows reduced activity and impaired functioning. This impairment leads to poor decision-making, difficulty in resisting impulses, and an inability to weigh the long-term consequences of their actions.

The reduced activity in the prefrontal cortex also contributes to the loss of control over gambling behavior. Compulsive gamblers often find it challenging to stop gambling once they have started, and they may continue to gamble despite experiencing significant losses and negative outcomes.

The Role of Stress and Anxiety:

STRESS AND ANXIETY can exacerbate gambling addiction by further impairing the brain's decision-making and impulse control capabilities. When individuals experience stress or anxiety, the brain's ability to regulate emotions and make rational decisions becomes compromised. As a result, they may turn to gambling as a way to cope with these negative emotions, creating a vicious cycle of addiction.

Additionally, the act of gambling itself can induce stress and anxiety, particularly when individuals experience losses or financial strain. This heightened state of arousal further impairs the brain's ability to make rational decisions and resist the urge to gamble.

The Cycle of Addiction:

THE COMBINATION OF a hypersensitive reward system, impaired prefrontal cortex functioning, and heightened stress and anxiety creates a cycle of addiction that is difficult to break. Compulsive gamblers become trapped in a loop where the anticipation and excitement of gambling drive them to continue, while the negative consequences and impaired decision-making perpetuate the behavior.

Breaking this cycle requires a comprehensive approach that addresses both the psychological and physiological aspects of the disorder. Understanding how gambling affects the brain is a crucial step in developing effective treatment strategies and supporting individuals on their journey to recovery.

Moving Forward

IN THIS CHAPTER, WE have explored the definition and types of gambling addiction, the psychological and physiological factors that contribute to compulsive gambling, and how gambling affects the brain. This foundational knowledge is essential for understanding the complexity of gambling addiction and the challenges faced by those who struggle with this disorder.

As we move forward in this book, we will delve deeper into the various aspects of compulsive gambling and provide practical strategies for overcoming this addiction. By raising awareness, offering education, and providing support, we aim to empower individuals to break free from the grip of gambling and reclaim their lives.

Recovery from compulsive gambling is a journey that requires patience, commitment, and support. Whether you are personally struggling with gambling addiction or supporting someone who is, know that help is available, and recovery is possible. Together, we can build a brighter future free from the destructive impact of compulsive gambling.

Chapter 2: Recognizing the Signs

Early Warning Signs of Gambling Addiction

Recognizing the early warning signs of gambling addiction is crucial in preventing the disorder from escalating to a stage where it becomes significantly more challenging to manage. Early intervention can make a profound difference in the trajectory of the disorder, offering a greater chance of recovery. The early signs of gambling addiction can often be subtle and easily overlooked, particularly because gambling is socially acceptable and widely promoted. However, being aware of these signs can help individuals and their loved ones identify the problem before it spirals out of control.

1. Preoccupation with Gambling:

ONE OF THE EARLIEST signs of gambling addiction is an increased preoccupation with gambling. This can manifest as constantly thinking about past gambling experiences, planning the next gambling opportunity, or strategizing on how to get money for gambling. An individual may frequently talk about gambling or become unusually interested in the outcomes of sporting events, lotteries, or other gambling activities.

2. Increased Tolerance:

AS WITH OTHER ADDICTIONS, individuals with gambling addiction often develop a tolerance to the activity. This means that they need to gamble with larger amounts of money or take bigger risks to achieve the same level of excitement or thrill that they initially experienced. Increased tolerance can lead to more frequent gambling sessions and higher stakes, which in turn increases the potential for significant financial losses.

3. Chasing Losses:

A HALLMARK OF GAMBLING addiction is the compulsion to chase losses. When individuals lose money gambling, they may feel an intense need to continue gambling in an attempt to win back the money they have lost. This often leads to even greater losses and perpetuates the cycle of addiction. Chasing losses is a dangerous behavior that can quickly escalate into significant financial and emotional distress.

4. Lying and Deception:

AS GAMBLING BEHAVIOR becomes more problematic, individuals often begin to lie or deceive others about their gambling activities. They may hide the extent of their gambling from family and friends, lie about how much money they have lost, or cover up the time spent gambling. This deception can strain relationships and lead to feelings of guilt and shame.

5. Borrowing Money or Financial Problems:

FINANCIAL DIFFICULTIES are a common early sign of gambling addiction. Individuals may begin to borrow money from friends, family, or even take out loans to fund their gambling. They might also sell personal belongings or neglect financial obligations such as bills and debts. As financial problems worsen, individuals may become increasingly desperate, leading to more reckless gambling behavior.

6. Neglecting Responsibilities:

ANOTHER EARLY WARNING sign of gambling addiction is the neglect of personal and professional responsibilities. Individuals may start to miss work, school, or important family events because of their gambling activities. Their performance at work or school may decline, and they may lose interest in hobbies or activities they once enjoyed.

7. Emotional Changes:

EMOTIONAL CHANGES ARE often an early indicator of gambling addiction. Individuals may become more irritable, anxious, or depressed as their gambling behavior escalates. They may also experience mood swings, becoming euphoric after a win and despondent after a loss. These emotional changes can have a significant impact on relationships and overall well-being.

Behavioral, Emotional, and Physical Indicators

IN ADDITION TO THE early warning signs, gambling addiction can manifest through various behavioral, emotional, and physical indicators. Recognizing these indicators can help individuals and their loved ones identify the presence of a gambling problem and take appropriate action.

Behavioral Indicators:

1. SECRECY AND ISOLATION:

Individuals with gambling addiction often become secretive about their activities and isolate themselves from family and friends. They may spend increasing amounts of time alone, either gambling or thinking about gambling. This secrecy and isolation can lead to a breakdown in relationships and a lack of social support.

2. Neglecting Personal Hygiene and Appearance:

As gambling becomes the primary focus of their lives, individuals may neglect their personal hygiene and appearance. They may show up to work or social events looking disheveled or unkempt, which can be a noticeable change from their usual behavior.

3. Frequent Absences:

Frequent absences from work, school, or social commitments can be a significant behavioral indicator of gambling addiction. Individuals may call in sick, leave early, or simply disappear for extended periods to gamble. This behavior can lead to job loss, academic failure, and strained relationships.

4. Increased Risk-Taking:

Gambling addiction often leads to increased risk-taking behavior. Individuals may engage in more reckless gambling activities, such as betting larger amounts of money, participating in illegal gambling, or using credit cards to fund their gambling. This risk-taking can result in severe financial and legal consequences.

Emotional Indicators:

1. MOOD SWINGS:

Individuals with gambling addiction often experience significant mood swings. They may feel euphoric and energized after a win, only to become irritable, anxious, or depressed after a loss. These mood swings can affect their interactions with others and contribute to relationship problems.

2. Guilt and Shame:

Feelings of guilt and shame are common among individuals with gambling addiction. They may feel ashamed of their behavior, particularly if they have lied or deceived others about their gambling. This guilt and shame can contribute to a cycle of negative emotions and further gambling.

3. Anxiety and Depression:

Anxiety and depression are prevalent among individuals with gambling addiction. The stress of financial problems, relationship issues, and the compulsion to gamble can lead to chronic anxiety and depression. These emotional states can further fuel the addiction as individuals may gamble to escape their negative feelings.

4. Restlessness and Irritability:

Restlessness and irritability are also common emotional indicators of gambling addiction. Individuals may become agitated or short-tempered when they are unable to gamble or when they are thinking about gambling. This restlessness can affect their ability to focus on other tasks and contribute to conflicts with others.

Physical Indicators:

1. SLEEP PROBLEMS:

Gambling addiction can lead to significant disruptions in sleep patterns. Individuals may stay up late or wake up early to gamble, leading to sleep deprivation. This lack of sleep can result in physical fatigue, difficulty concentrating, and decreased overall health.

2. Weight Changes:

Weight changes, either weight loss or weight gain, can be a physical indicator of gambling addiction. Some individuals may neglect their nutritional needs due to the time and money spent on gambling, leading to weight loss. Others may engage in stress eating, resulting in weight gain.

3. Physical Health Issues:

Chronic stress associated with gambling addiction can lead to various physical health issues, such as headaches, stomach problems, and high blood pressure. The physical toll of stress can further impact an individual's overall well-being and quality of life.

4. Substance Abuse:

Substance abuse is often co-occurring with gambling addiction. Individuals may turn to drugs or alcohol to cope with the emotional and physical stress of their gambling behavior. Substance abuse can exacerbate the addiction and lead to additional health and legal problems.

Self-Assessment Tools

RECOGNIZING THE SIGNS of gambling addiction is the first step toward recovery. Self-assessment tools can help individuals evaluate their gambling behavior and determine whether they may have a problem. These tools are designed to prompt self-reflection and encourage individuals to seek help if necessary.

1. Gamblers Anonymous Twenty Questions:

Gamblers Anonymous, a support group for individuals with gambling addiction, has developed a list of twenty questions to help individuals assess their gambling behavior. Answering "yes" to seven or more of these questions suggests that the individual may have a gambling problem and should seek help.

2. Diagnostic Criteria for Gambling Disorder:

The Diagnostic and Statistical Manual of Mental Disorders (DSM-5) outlines criteria for diagnosing gambling disorder. These criteria include:

- Need to gamble with increasing amounts of money to achieve the desired excitement.

- Restlessness or irritability when attempting to cut down or stop gambling.

- Repeated unsuccessful efforts to control, cut back, or stop gambling.

- Preoccupation with gambling.

- Gambling as a way to escape from problems or relieve feelings of helplessness, guilt, anxiety, or depression.

- Chasing losses.

- Lying to conceal the extent of gambling involvement.

- Jeopardizing or losing significant relationships, jobs, or educational/career opportunities because of gambling.

- Relying on others to provide money to relieve desperate financial situations caused by gambling.

Meeting four or more of these criteria within a 12-month period indicates a gambling disorder.

3. South Oaks Gambling Screen (SOGS):

The South Oaks Gambling Screen (SOGS) is a widely used screening tool that helps identify individuals with potential gambling problems. The SOGS consists of a series of questions about gambling behavior, financial losses, and the impact of gambling on the individual's life. A higher score on the SOGS indicates a greater likelihood of having a gambling problem.

4. Lie/Bet Questionnaire:

The Lie/Bet Questionnaire is a simple two-question screening tool designed to identify individuals with potential gambling problems. The questions are:

- Have you ever felt the need to bet more and more money?

- Have you ever had to lie to people important to you about how much you gambled?

Answering "yes" to either question suggests that the individual may have a gambling problem and should seek further assessment and help.

5. NODS-CLiP:

The NODS-CLiP is a brief screening tool derived from the National Opinion Research Center DSM-IV Screen for Gambling Problems (NODS). It consists of three questions:

- Have you ever tried to cut down on your gambling?

- Have people annoyed you by criticizing your gambling?

- Have you ever felt guilty about the way you gamble or what happens when you gamble?

Answering "yes" to any of these questions suggests that the individual may have a gambling problem and should seek further assessment and help.

6. Online Self-Assessment Tools:

Several online self-assessment tools are available to help individuals evaluate their gambling behavior. These tools often consist of a series of questions about gambling frequency, financial losses, emotional impact, and other relevant factors. Examples of online self-assessment tools include those provided by the National Council on Problem Gambling and other reputable organizations.

Taking Action

RECOGNIZING THE SIGNS of gambling addiction is a critical step in addressing the problem. If you or someone you know exhibits any of the early warning signs, behavioral, emotional, or physical indicators discussed in this chapter, it is essential to take action.

1. Seek Professional Help:

Professional help, such as therapy or counseling, can provide valuable support and guidance in addressing gambling addiction. Cognitive-behavioral therapy (CBT), in particular, has been shown to be effective in treating gambling disorder. A therapist can help individuals identify the underlying causes of their gambling behavior, develop coping strategies, and work towards recovery.

2. Join a Support Group:

Support groups, such as Gamblers Anonymous, offer a safe and supportive environment for individuals with gambling addiction to share their experiences and receive encouragement from others who understand their struggles. Support groups can provide a sense of community and accountability, which is essential for recovery.

3. Develop a Support System:

Building a support system of family, friends, and trusted individuals can provide emotional and practical support during the recovery process. Open and honest communication with loved ones can help rebuild trust and strengthen relationships.

4. Financial Management:

Addressing the financial impact of gambling addiction is crucial. Working with a financial advisor or credit counselor can help individuals develop a plan to manage their debts and rebuild their financial stability.

5. Implement Healthy Habits:

Replacing gambling with positive activities and hobbies can help individuals find fulfillment and reduce the urge to gamble. Engaging in physical exercise, mindfulness practices, and other stress-relief techniques can support overall well-being.

6. Set Goals:

Setting realistic and achievable goals can provide motivation and a sense of purpose during the recovery process. Celebrating small milestones and achievements can reinforce positive behavior and encourage continued progress.

Moving Forward

IN THIS CHAPTER, WE have explored the early warning signs of gambling addiction, as well as the behavioral, emotional, and physical indicators that can help identify the presence of a gambling problem. Recognizing these signs is the first step towards addressing gambling addiction and seeking help.

Self-assessment tools can provide valuable insights into an individual's gambling behavior and help determine whether professional help is needed. Taking action by seeking therapy, joining support groups, developing a support system, managing finances, implementing healthy habits, and setting goals can significantly aid in the recovery process.

Gambling addiction is a challenging disorder, but recovery is possible with the right support and strategies. By recognizing the signs and taking proactive steps, individuals can break free from the grip of gambling addiction and work towards a healthier, more fulfilling life.

As we move forward in this book, we will continue to explore various aspects of gambling addiction and provide practical strategies for overcoming this disorder. Together, we can build a brighter future free from the destructive impact of compulsive gambling.

Chapter 3: The Impact of Gambling Addiction

Gambling addiction, often referred to as pathological gambling, has far-reaching impacts that extend beyond the individual suffering from the disorder. The consequences of compulsive gambling can be devastating, affecting financial stability, relationships, family life, and both mental and physical health. Understanding these impacts is crucial for recognizing the severity of the disorder and the importance of seeking help.

Financial Consequences

ONE OF THE MOST IMMEDIATE and noticeable impacts of gambling addiction is financial devastation. Compulsive gamblers often engage in behaviors that lead to significant monetary losses, which can have long-term repercussions on their financial well-being.

1. Depletion of Savings and Assets:

Compulsive gamblers frequently exhaust their savings in an attempt to fund their gambling activities. This depletion of savings can lead to the liquidation of assets, such as cars, homes, and other valuable possessions. The loss of these assets can create a financial crisis and leave individuals without a safety net.

2. Accumulation of Debt:

As savings run dry, many gamblers turn to borrowing money to continue gambling. This often leads to the accumulation of substantial debt, including personal loans, credit card debt, and payday loans with exorbitant interest rates. The debt can quickly become unmanageable, leading to financial instability and potential bankruptcy.

3. Employment Issues:

The compulsion to gamble can interfere with an individual's ability to maintain stable employment. Gamblers may miss work, perform poorly on the job, or even steal from their employers to fund their addiction. These behaviors can result in job loss, further exacerbating financial difficulties and reducing the ability to repay debt.

4. Legal Problems:

In some cases, individuals may resort to illegal activities to obtain money for gambling. This can include theft, fraud, or embezzlement, which can lead to criminal charges, legal fees, and potential incarceration. The legal consequences can have a lasting impact on an individual's financial and personal life.

5. Impact on Credit Scores:

The financial mismanagement associated with gambling addiction often results in missed bill payments, defaulted loans, and maxed-out credit cards. These actions can severely damage an individual's credit score, making it difficult to secure loans, rent housing, or obtain employment in the future.

6. Family Financial Stress:

The financial strain of gambling addiction extends to the individual's family. Spouses, children, and other family members may experience financial stress and uncertainty as a result of the gambler's behavior. This can lead to a reduction in quality of life, inability to afford basic necessities, and significant emotional distress.

Effects on Relationships and Family Life

THE IMPACT OF GAMBLING addiction on relationships and family life is profound. The deception, financial strain, and emotional turmoil caused by the addiction can lead to a breakdown in trust and communication, ultimately damaging or destroying relationships.

1. Loss of Trust:

Trust is a fundamental component of any healthy relationship. Gambling addiction often involves lying and deception, as individuals hide their gambling activities and financial losses from their loved ones. The discovery of these lies can lead to a significant loss of trust, which is difficult to rebuild.

2. Strain on Marriages:

Marital relationships are particularly vulnerable to the effects of gambling addiction. The financial strain, emotional volatility, and loss of trust can create an environment of constant conflict and tension. Many marriages struggle to survive the impact of gambling addiction, leading to separation or divorce in many cases.

3. Impact on Children:

Children of compulsive gamblers often suffer the consequences of their parent's addiction. They may experience emotional neglect, financial instability, and exposure to conflict and stress within the home. These experiences can have long-term effects on their emotional and psychological development.

4. Isolation and Estrangement:

Gambling addiction can lead to social isolation and estrangement from friends and family. Individuals may withdraw from social activities and relationships to focus on gambling. Friends and family may also distance themselves due to the negative impact of the gambler's behavior, leaving the individual without a support network.

5. Co-Dependency and Enabling:

In some cases, family members may become co-dependent or enable the gambler's behavior. This can include covering up for the gambler, providing financial support, or making excuses for their actions. While often well-intentioned, these behaviors can perpetuate the addiction and delay recovery.

6. Domestic Violence and Abuse:

The stress and tension associated with gambling addiction can sometimes escalate into domestic violence or abuse. This can include physical, emotional, or verbal abuse directed at family members. The presence of such violence creates an unsafe and unhealthy home environment.

Mental and Physical Health Repercussions

THE MENTAL AND PHYSICAL health repercussions of gambling addiction are significant and can further complicate the individual's ability to recover. The stress and emotional turmoil associated with the addiction take a toll on both mental and physical well-being.

1. Mental Health Disorders:

Gambling addiction is often accompanied by other mental health disorders, such as depression, anxiety, and substance abuse. The constant stress and emotional ups and downs of gambling can exacerbate these conditions, leading to a cycle of worsening mental health and increased gambling behavior.

- Depression: The financial losses, relationship problems, and sense of hopelessness associated with gambling addiction can lead to severe depression. Individuals may feel trapped in their situation and unable to see a way out, which can contribute to suicidal thoughts or behaviors.

- Anxiety: The constant worry about money, hiding gambling activities, and fear of being discovered can create chronic anxiety. This anxiety can interfere with daily functioning and further drive the compulsion to gamble as a means of escape.

- Substance Abuse: Many individuals with gambling addiction also struggle with substance abuse. Alcohol and drugs may be used to cope with the stress and emotional pain of gambling losses, creating a dangerous combination of addictions that are challenging to treat.

2. Emotional Instability:

The emotional rollercoaster of gambling addiction can lead to significant instability. Winning can produce feelings of euphoria and invincibility, while losing can result in deep despair and self-loathing. These extreme emotional swings can impact relationships and overall mental health.

3. Physical Health Problems:

The stress associated with gambling addiction can manifest in various physical health problems. Chronic stress can lead to headaches, gastrointestinal issues, high blood pressure, and weakened immune function. The physical toll of stress can also contribute to more serious health conditions over time.

4. Sleep Disturbances:

Gambling addiction often leads to irregular sleep patterns and sleep disturbances. Individuals may stay up late gambling, experience difficulty falling asleep due to anxiety, or wake up early to gamble. Chronic sleep deprivation can have significant negative effects on physical and mental health.

5. Poor Nutrition and Neglect of Self-Care:

The compulsion to gamble can result in neglect of self-care, including poor nutrition and lack of exercise. Individuals may skip meals, eat unhealthy foods, or forgo regular medical check-ups. This neglect of self-care can contribute to a decline in overall health and well-being.

6. Increased Risk of Cardiovascular Problems:

The stress and anxiety associated with gambling addiction can increase the risk of cardiovascular problems, such as heart attacks and strokes. The heightened emotional state during gambling, combined with the physical effects of chronic stress, can place significant strain on the cardiovascular system.

7. Impact on Cognitive Functioning:

Gambling addiction can also impact cognitive functioning, leading to difficulties with concentration, decision-making, and memory. The preoccupation with gambling and the stress of managing the addiction can impair cognitive abilities, making it challenging to perform everyday tasks or make sound decisions.

Comprehensive Approach to Recovery

UNDERSTANDING THE MULTIFACETED impact of gambling addiction highlights the importance of a comprehensive approach to recovery. Addressing the financial, relational, and health consequences requires a combination of strategies and support systems.

1. Financial Counseling and Management:

Financial counseling can help individuals develop a plan to manage their debts, create a budget, and rebuild their financial stability. Working with a financial advisor or credit counselor can provide practical guidance and support in navigating the financial challenges associated with gambling addiction.

2. Therapy and Counseling:

Therapy, particularly cognitive-behavioral therapy (CBT), is effective in addressing the underlying psychological factors contributing to gambling addiction. Therapy can help individuals identify triggers, develop coping strategies, and work through emotional issues related to the addiction.

3. Support Groups:

Support groups, such as Gamblers Anonymous, offer a community of individuals who understand the challenges of gambling addiction. These groups provide a safe space for sharing experiences, receiving support, and finding accountability. The sense of community and shared understanding can be invaluable in the recovery process.

4. Relationship Counseling:

Relationship counseling can help repair the damage caused by gambling addiction. Couples therapy or family therapy can address issues of trust, communication, and emotional support. Rebuilding relationships and creating a supportive home environment are critical components of recovery.

5. Health and Wellness:

Focusing on health and wellness is essential in the recovery process. Regular exercise, a balanced diet, and adequate sleep can support physical health and improve overall well-being. Incorporating stress-relief techniques, such as mindfulness or meditation, can also help manage the emotional impact of gambling addiction.

6. Developing Healthy Habits:

Replacing gambling with positive activities and hobbies can provide fulfillment and reduce the urge to gamble. Engaging in new interests, socializing with supportive friends, and pursuing personal goals can contribute to a sense of purpose and satisfaction.

7. Education and Awareness:

Education and awareness about the nature of gambling addiction and its consequences are crucial for both individuals and their loved ones. Understanding the disorder can reduce stigma, promote empathy, and encourage open conversations about seeking help.

Moving Forward

THE IMPACT OF GAMBLING addiction is profound and far-reaching, affecting financial stability, relationships, and both mental and physical health. Recognizing the severity of these consequences underscores the importance of seeking help and pursuing recovery.

Recovery from gambling addiction is a challenging journey, but it is possible with the right support and strategies. Addressing the financial, relational, and health impacts requires a comprehensive approach that includes professional counseling, support groups, financial management, and a focus on overall well-being.

As we move forward in this book, we will continue to explore various aspects of gambling addiction and provide practical strategies for overcoming this disorder. By understanding the impact of gambling addiction and taking proactive steps, individuals can break free from the grip of gambling and work towards a healthier, more fulfilling life.

Together, we can build a brighter future free from the destructive impact of compulsive gambling. Whether you are personally struggling with gambling addiction or supporting someone who is, know that help is available and recovery is possible. Let us take the next step forward on this journey towards healing and recovery.

Chapter 4: The Psychology Behind Gambling

The Thrill of Risk-Taking

The allure of gambling can be deeply rooted in the psychology of risk-taking. For many, the excitement of betting and the possibility of winning create a powerful rush. Understanding the psychological mechanisms behind this thrill is crucial to grasp why gambling can become addictive.

1. The Dopamine Rush:

Gambling activates the brain's reward system, particularly involving the neurotransmitter dopamine. Dopamine is associated with pleasure and reward, and its release reinforces behaviors that are perceived as enjoyable. When individuals gamble, the anticipation of a potential win triggers a surge of dopamine, creating feelings of excitement and euphoria. This dopamine rush is akin to the highs experienced with other addictive behaviors, such as drug use.

The unpredictability and uncertainty of gambling outcomes further amplify this effect. The brain finds random, intermittent rewards particularly compelling, making gambling highly addictive. The occasional wins, even when interspersed with losses, keep the dopamine system engaged and drive individuals to continue gambling in pursuit of the next high.

2. Sensation-Seeking and Personality Traits:

Certain personality traits, such as sensation-seeking, impulsivity, and a need for excitement, make individuals more prone to gambling addiction. Sensation-seekers are individuals who crave novel and intense experiences. Gambling provides a perfect outlet for these desires, as it offers high stakes, unpredictability, and the potential for significant rewards.

Impulsivity, characterized by acting on whims without considering consequences, is another trait commonly associated with gambling addiction.

Impulsive individuals are more likely to engage in risky behaviors, including gambling, without fully considering the potential negative outcomes.

3. The Illusion of Control:

A psychological phenomenon known as the illusion of control plays a significant role in gambling behavior. This cognitive bias leads individuals to believe they can influence or control outcomes that are inherently random. Gamblers often perceive themselves as having skill or strategy in games of chance, which reinforces their belief in their ability to win.

For example, gamblers may develop superstitious behaviors or rituals they believe will improve their odds of winning. They might also attribute wins to their skills while dismissing losses as bad luck or external factors. This illusion of control can perpetuate gambling behavior, as individuals continue to believe that their next win is just around the corner.

4. The Role of Competition:

For many gamblers, especially those engaged in skill-based games like poker or sports betting, the competitive aspect of gambling is a significant draw. The desire to outsmart opponents, prove oneself, and emerge victorious can be highly motivating. This competitive drive can lead to prolonged gambling sessions and higher stakes, as individuals strive to achieve their next win.

5. The Near-Miss Effect:

The near-miss effect is another psychological factor that contributes to the thrill of gambling. A near-miss occurs when the outcome of a gambling event is close to a win but ultimately results in a loss. For example, a slot machine might display two winning symbols and a third that is just off, creating a sense of being "so close" to winning.

Near-misses activate the brain's reward system similarly to actual wins, despite not resulting in a payout. This phenomenon keeps gamblers engaged and motivated to continue playing, as they feel that a win is within reach.

The Role of Escapism and Stress Relief

FOR MANY INDIVIDUALS, gambling serves as a means of escapism and stress relief. Understanding how gambling provides temporary respite from life's challenges can shed light on why some people turn to it as a coping mechanism.

1. Escaping from Reality:

Life's challenges, such as financial difficulties, relationship problems, work stress, or emotional pain, can drive individuals to seek escape. Gambling offers a temporary reprieve from these issues, allowing individuals to immerse themselves in the excitement and focus of the game. The casino environment, with its bright lights, sounds, and social interactions, provides a stark contrast to the mundane or stressful aspects of daily life.

2. Emotional Numbing:

Gambling can serve as a way to numb difficult emotions and avoid dealing with them. The intense focus required during gambling can distract individuals from feelings of sadness, anxiety, or loneliness. The highs and lows of gambling provide an emotional rollercoaster that temporarily overrides other emotional pain.

3. The Role of Boredom:

Boredom and a lack of stimulating activities can also drive individuals to gamble. For some, gambling provides excitement and a sense of purpose that might be missing in other areas of their lives. The thrill of betting and the anticipation of winning can fill a void created by boredom.

4. Social Interaction:

Gambling environments, such as casinos or online gaming communities, offer social interaction and a sense of belonging. For individuals who feel isolated or lonely, these social aspects can be appealing. Engaging with other gamblers, sharing experiences, and being part of a community can provide a sense of connection that might be lacking elsewhere.

5. Stress Relief:

The modern world is rife with stressors, from work pressures to personal responsibilities. Gambling can provide a temporary escape from these stressors and offer a way to relax. The act of placing bets and engaging in games can create a sense of control and mastery, even if it is illusory. This perceived control can be soothing in the face of life's uncertainties.

6. Coping with Trauma:

For some individuals, gambling serves as a coping mechanism for dealing with past trauma or unresolved emotional issues. The numbing effect of gambling and the distraction it provides can offer temporary relief from traumatic memories or unresolved pain. However, this form of escapism can be detrimental in the long run, as it prevents individuals from addressing and healing their underlying issues.

Understanding the Gambling Cycle

THE GAMBLING CYCLE refers to the pattern of behavior that characterizes gambling addiction. This cycle is self-perpetuating and can be difficult to break without intervention. Understanding the stages of the gambling cycle can provide insight into how addiction develops and persists.

1. The Winning Phase:

The gambling cycle often begins with a winning phase, where individuals experience initial success and excitement. The thrill of winning and the associated dopamine rush create positive reinforcement, encouraging continued gambling. During this phase, individuals may feel euphoric, confident, and in control.

- Increased Gambling: The early wins lead to increased gambling behavior, as individuals seek to replicate their success and experience the same high. They may start betting larger amounts of money and engaging in more frequent gambling sessions.

- Rationalization: Gamblers rationalize their behavior by believing they have developed skills or strategies that increase their chances of winning. The illusion of control reinforces their confidence and commitment to gambling.

2. The Losing Phase:

The losing phase follows the initial winning phase and is characterized by a series of losses. As individuals continue to gamble, the odds inevitably catch up with them, resulting in financial losses. The emotional impact of losing can be profound, leading to frustration, anger, and despair.

- Chasing Losses: During the losing phase, individuals often engage in "chasing losses." This behavior involves continuing to gamble in an attempt to win back lost money. The compulsion to chase losses is driven by the belief that a big win is just around the corner and will make up for previous losses.

- Desperation: The financial strain and emotional distress of losing can lead to desperation. Individuals may take greater risks, borrow money, or engage in illegal activities to fund their gambling. The cycle of losses and attempts to recoup them perpetuates the addiction.

3. The Desperation Phase:

The desperation phase is marked by a significant escalation in gambling behavior and its consequences. Individuals in this phase may feel trapped in their addiction and unable to stop despite the negative impact on their lives.

- Isolation: As the addiction worsens, individuals may isolate themselves from family and friends. The secrecy and shame associated with gambling can lead to withdrawal from social activities and relationships.

- Neglect of Responsibilities: The compulsion to gamble can result in the neglect of personal and professional responsibilities. Individuals may miss work, fail to pay bills, and neglect their health and well-being.

- Emotional and Physical Deterioration: The stress and emotional turmoil of the desperation phase can lead to mental health issues, such as depression and anxiety. Physical health may also decline due to poor nutrition, lack of sleep, and increased stress.

4. The Hopelessness Phase:

The hopelessness phase represents the culmination of the gambling cycle, where individuals feel a sense of hopelessness and despair. The consequences of gambling addiction become overwhelming, and the individual may feel that there is no way out.

- Acknowledgment of Addiction: In this phase, individuals may begin to recognize the severity of their addiction and its impact on their lives. The realization that gambling is no longer a source of pleasure but a destructive force can be sobering.

- Seeking Help: For some, the hopelessness phase serves as a turning point where they seek help and support. Recognizing the need for intervention and reaching out for assistance is a critical step towards recovery.

- Relapse and Recovery: Even after seeking help, individuals may experience relapses. Recovery from gambling addiction is a process that involves ongoing effort and support. Understanding the gambling cycle and the factors that drive it can help individuals develop strategies to break free from its grip.

Breaking the Gambling Cycle

BREAKING THE GAMBLING cycle requires a multifaceted approach that addresses the psychological, emotional, and behavioral aspects of addiction. Successful recovery involves understanding the underlying factors that drive gambling behavior and developing strategies to overcome them.

1. Cognitive-Behavioral Therapy (CBT):

Cognitive-behavioral therapy (CBT) is an effective treatment for gambling addiction. CBT helps individuals identify and challenge distorted thoughts and beliefs related to gambling. By recognizing cognitive biases, such as the illusion of control and the gambler's fallacy, individuals can develop healthier thinking patterns and reduce the compulsion to gamble.

CBT also focuses on developing coping strategies to manage stress and negative emotions without resorting to gambling. Techniques such as mindfulness, relaxation exercises, and problem-solving skills can help individuals navigate life's challenges more effectively.

2. Building a Support System:

A strong support system is essential for recovery from gambling addiction. Family, friends, and support groups can provide encouragement, accountability, and understanding. Engaging with others who have experienced similar struggles can create a sense of community and reduce feelings of isolation.

Support groups, such as Gamblers Anonymous, offer a structured program for recovery that includes regular meetings, peer support, and a focus on personal growth. The shared experiences and insights of group members can be invaluable in the recovery process.

3. Financial Counseling:

Addressing the financial consequences of gambling addiction is a critical component of recovery. Financial counseling can help individuals develop a plan to manage debt, create a budget, and rebuild their financial stability. Working with a financial advisor or credit counselor can provide practical guidance and support in navigating financial challenges.

4. Developing Healthy Habits:

Replacing gambling with positive activities and hobbies can provide fulfillment and reduce the urge to gamble. Engaging in new interests, socializing with supportive friends, and pursuing personal goals can contribute to a sense of purpose and satisfaction.

Physical exercise, mindfulness practices, and other stress-relief techniques can support overall well-being and reduce the reliance on gambling as a coping mechanism.

5. Setting Goals:

Setting realistic and achievable goals can provide motivation and a sense of purpose during the recovery process. Celebrating small milestones and achievements can reinforce positive behavior and encourage continued progress.

6. Education and Awareness:

Education and awareness about the nature of gambling addiction and its consequences are crucial for both individuals and their loved ones. Understanding the disorder can reduce stigma, promote empathy, and encourage open conversations about seeking help.

Moving Forward

THE PSYCHOLOGY BEHIND gambling addiction is complex, involving the thrill of risk-taking, the role of escapism and stress relief, and the cyclical nature of the addiction. Recognizing these psychological factors is essential for understanding why gambling can become so compelling and difficult to overcome.

Breaking the gambling cycle requires a comprehensive approach that addresses the underlying psychological, emotional, and behavioral aspects of addiction. By seeking professional help, building a support system, addressing financial challenges, and developing healthy habits, individuals can work towards recovery and a healthier, more fulfilling life.

As we continue to explore the various aspects of gambling addiction in this book, we will provide practical strategies and insights to support individuals on their journey to recovery. Understanding the psychology behind gambling is a crucial step in this process, as it equips individuals with the knowledge and tools needed to break free from the grip of addiction.

Together, we can build a brighter future free from the destructive impact of compulsive gambling. Whether you are personally struggling with gambling addiction or supporting someone who is, know that help is available and recovery is possible. Let us take the next step forward on this journey towards healing and recovery.

Chapter 5: Breaking the Denial

———

Breaking the cycle of gambling addiction often begins with overcoming denial. Denial is a powerful psychological defense mechanism that allows individuals to avoid acknowledging the reality of their situation. For those struggling with gambling addiction, denial can manifest as minimizing the severity of their problem, rationalizing their behavior, or outright refusing to recognize their addiction. This chapter explores the complex emotions of shame and guilt, the importance of accepting the problem, and the crucial step of seeking help.

Overcoming Shame and Guilt

SHAME AND GUILT ARE common and powerful emotions experienced by individuals with gambling addiction. These feelings can be overwhelming and paralyzing, often contributing to the cycle of denial and addiction. Understanding and addressing these emotions is a crucial step in the recovery process.

1. Understanding Shame and Guilt:

Shame and guilt, while related, are distinct emotions. Guilt arises from the belief that one has done something wrong or harmful, often leading to feelings of remorse and a desire to make amends. In contrast, shame is a more pervasive and destructive emotion, involving a negative self-assessment. Individuals who feel shame believe that they are inherently flawed or worthless.

For gamblers, guilt may stem from specific actions, such as lying to loved ones, borrowing money, or neglecting responsibilities. Shame, on the other hand, is often linked to the perception that their addiction is a personal failure or a sign of moral weakness.

2. The Role of Society and Stigma:

Societal stigma around gambling addiction can exacerbate feelings of shame and guilt. Many people view addiction as a lack of willpower or a moral failing rather than recognizing it as a complex and multifaceted disorder. This stigma can lead to self-blame and further denial, making it difficult for individuals to seek help.

3. The Impact on Mental Health:

The burden of shame and guilt can have severe consequences for mental health. These emotions can lead to depression, anxiety, and low self-esteem, which can, in turn, fuel the addiction as individuals gamble to escape their negative feelings. Addressing these emotions is critical for breaking the cycle of addiction.

4. Strategies for Overcoming Shame and Guilt:

- Self-Compassion: Developing self-compassion involves treating oneself with the same kindness and understanding that one would offer to a friend. It means recognizing that everyone makes mistakes and that these mistakes do not define one's worth. Self-compassion can reduce the intensity of shame and guilt, making it easier to confront the addiction.

- Forgiveness: Forgiving oneself is a crucial step in overcoming shame and guilt. This involves acknowledging past mistakes, understanding their impact, and making a conscious decision to move forward without being weighed down by them. Forgiveness is not about excusing harmful behavior but about releasing the hold that guilt and shame have on one's life.

- Therapy: Professional therapy can provide a safe space to explore and address feelings of shame and guilt. Cognitive-behavioral therapy (CBT) and other therapeutic approaches can help individuals reframe negative thoughts and develop healthier coping mechanisms.

- Sharing Stories: Connecting with others who have experienced similar struggles can be incredibly validating. Support groups, such as Gamblers Anonymous, offer a community where individuals can share their stories, receive empathy, and realize they are not alone in their experiences.

Accepting the Problem

ACCEPTANCE IS A PIVOTAL step in the recovery process. It involves acknowledging the reality of the addiction and the impact it has had on one's life. This acceptance is not about self-condemnation but about recognizing the need for change and taking responsibility for one's actions.

1. The Role of Denial:

Denial is a common response to the realization that one has a problem. It serves as a protective mechanism to avoid the pain and discomfort associated with acknowledging the addiction. Denial can take various forms, such as minimizing the severity of the problem, blaming external factors, or rationalizing gambling behavior.

2. Breaking Through Denial:

- Self-Reflection: Taking time to reflect on one's behavior and its consequences is essential for breaking through denial. This reflection can be facilitated by keeping a journal, which helps track gambling activities, associated emotions, and the impact on daily life.

- Feedback from Others: Listening to feedback from trusted friends and family members can provide valuable insights. Loved ones often notice changes in behavior and the impact of gambling before the individual does. Their observations and concerns can help challenge denial and prompt acceptance.

- Recognizing Patterns: Identifying patterns in gambling behavior and their consequences can help individuals see the extent of their addiction. This includes acknowledging financial losses, strained relationships, and neglected responsibilities.

- Understanding Triggers: Recognizing the triggers that lead to gambling can aid in acceptance. Understanding what drives the compulsion to gamble, whether it's stress, boredom, or emotional distress, is crucial for developing strategies to manage these triggers.

3. The Role of Motivation:

Motivation plays a significant role in moving from denial to acceptance. The motivation to change can come from various sources, such as the desire to repair relationships, improve financial stability, or regain control of one's life. Identifying and cultivating these motivations can strengthen the commitment to recovery.

4. The Stages of Change Model:

The Stages of Change Model, developed by Prochaska and DiClemente, outlines the process of behavioral change. Understanding these stages can help individuals navigate the journey from denial to acceptance and beyond.

- Precontemplation: In this stage, individuals are not yet aware of their problem or the need for change. Denial is prevalent, and there is little to no intention of addressing the addiction.

- Contemplation: In this stage, individuals begin to recognize the problem and consider the possibility of change. They may weigh the pros and cons of their behavior but are not yet ready to take action.

- Preparation: In the preparation stage, individuals decide to take action and start planning for change. This might involve researching treatment options, setting goals, and seeking support.

- Action: In the action stage, individuals actively implement their plan to change their behavior. This can include attending therapy, joining support groups, and making lifestyle adjustments.

- Maintenance: The maintenance stage involves sustaining the changes made during the action stage and working to prevent relapse. Individuals develop strategies to cope with challenges and continue their progress.

- Relapse: Relapse is a common part of the recovery process. It involves returning to old behaviors after a period of abstinence. Recognizing relapse as a part of the journey rather than a failure can help individuals learn from their experiences and recommit to their recovery.

Importance of Seeking Help

SEEKING HELP IS A CRITICAL step in breaking the cycle of gambling addiction. Professional support, coupled with the understanding and encouragement of loved ones, can provide the tools and resources needed for successful recovery.

1. Professional Therapy:

Professional therapy is a cornerstone of effective treatment for gambling addiction. Therapists trained in addiction treatment can help individuals explore the underlying causes of their behavior, develop coping strategies, and work towards recovery.

- Cognitive-Behavioral Therapy (CBT): CBT is one of the most effective therapeutic approaches for gambling addiction. It focuses on identifying and challenging distorted thoughts and beliefs related to gambling. CBT helps individuals develop healthier thinking patterns and coping mechanisms.

- Motivational Interviewing: Motivational interviewing is a therapeutic approach that helps individuals resolve ambivalence about change. It involves exploring the individual's motivations for change and enhancing their commitment to recovery.

- Psychodynamic Therapy: Psychodynamic therapy explores the underlying emotional and psychological factors that contribute to gambling addiction. This approach helps individuals gain insight into their behavior and address unresolved issues.

- Family Therapy: Family therapy can be beneficial for addressing the impact of gambling addiction on relationships and family dynamics. It involves working with family members to improve communication, rebuild trust, and develop a supportive environment for recovery.

2. Support Groups:

Support groups, such as Gamblers Anonymous (GA), provide a community of individuals who understand the challenges of gambling addiction. These groups offer a safe space to share experiences, receive support, and find accountability.

- 12-Step Programs: GA and other 12-step programs follow a structured approach to recovery. The steps involve admitting powerlessness over the addiction, seeking support from a higher power, making amends for past actions, and helping others in their recovery journey.

- Peer Support: The shared experiences of group members create a sense of camaraderie and mutual understanding. Peer support can provide encouragement, motivation, and practical advice for overcoming challenges.

3. Financial Counseling:

Addressing the financial impact of gambling addiction is essential for recovery. Financial counseling can help individuals develop a plan to manage debt, create a budget, and rebuild financial stability.

- Debt Management: Financial counselors can assist in negotiating with creditors, consolidating debt, and creating a manageable repayment plan. This can reduce financial stress and provide a clear path forward.

- Budgeting: Developing a realistic budget helps individuals track their income and expenses, prioritize essential costs, and avoid unnecessary spending. Budgeting tools and apps can provide additional support in managing finances.

- Financial Education: Learning about financial management, credit repair, and saving strategies can empower individuals to take control of their financial future. Financial education workshops and resources are often available through community organizations and counseling services.

4. Building a Support System:

A strong support system is crucial for recovery from gambling addiction. Family, friends, and trusted individuals can provide emotional support, encouragement, and accountability.

- Open Communication: Honest and open communication with loved ones is essential for rebuilding trust and maintaining a supportive environment. Sharing the challenges and progress of recovery can strengthen relationships and provide mutual understanding.

- Setting Boundaries: Establishing boundaries with family and friends can help create a healthy and supportive environment. This might include limiting discussions about gambling, avoiding enabling behaviors, and respecting each other's space and needs.

- Involving Loved Ones: Involving family and friends in the recovery process can provide additional motivation and support. Loved ones can participate in therapy sessions, attend support group meetings, and help create a structured and positive environment.

5. Developing Healthy Habits:

Replacing gambling with positive activities and hobbies can provide fulfillment and reduce the urge to gamble. Engaging in new interests, socializing with supportive friends, and pursuing personal goals can contribute to a sense of purpose and satisfaction.

- Physical Exercise: Regular physical exercise can improve overall well-being, reduce stress, and boost mood. Activities such as walking, running, yoga, or team sports can provide a healthy outlet for energy and emotions.

- Mindfulness Practices: Mindfulness practices, such as meditation and deep breathing exercises, can help individuals manage stress, improve focus, and develop greater self-awareness. Mindfulness can also enhance the ability to cope with cravings and urges.

- Hobbies and Interests: Exploring new hobbies and interests can provide a sense of accomplishment and enjoyment. Creative activities, such as painting, writing, or playing music, can offer a productive and fulfilling way to spend time.

6. Setting Goals:

Setting realistic and achievable goals can provide motivation and a sense of purpose during the recovery process. Goals can be related to various aspects of life, including financial stability, personal growth, relationships, and health.

- Short-Term Goals: Short-term goals are specific, achievable steps that can be accomplished in a relatively short period. Examples include attending therapy sessions, reducing gambling activities, or creating a budget.

- Long-Term Goals: Long-term goals are broader objectives that require sustained effort over time. Examples include achieving financial stability, rebuilding relationships, or maintaining abstinence from gambling.

- Tracking Progress: Keeping track of progress towards goals can provide a sense of accomplishment and motivation. Journaling, using goal-tracking apps, or sharing progress with a support group can help individuals stay focused and committed.

7. Education and Awareness:

Education and awareness about the nature of gambling addiction and its consequences are crucial for both individuals and their loved ones. Understanding the disorder can reduce stigma, promote empathy, and encourage open conversations about seeking help.

- Educational Resources: Books, articles, and online resources can provide valuable information about gambling addiction, its causes, and treatment options. Educational workshops and seminars can also offer insights and support.

- Awareness Campaigns: Community organizations and advocacy groups often run awareness campaigns to educate the public about gambling addiction. These campaigns can help reduce stigma, promote early intervention, and encourage individuals to seek help.

Moving Forward

BREAKING THE DENIAL associated with gambling addiction is a challenging but essential step towards recovery. Overcoming shame and guilt, accepting the problem, and seeking help are crucial components of this process. By addressing these emotional barriers and taking proactive steps, individuals can begin their journey towards healing and recovery.

As we continue to explore the various aspects of gambling addiction in this book, we will provide practical strategies and insights to support individuals on their path to recovery. Understanding the importance of breaking denial and seeking help is a crucial step in this process, as it equips individuals with the knowledge and tools needed to overcome addiction and rebuild their lives.

Together, we can build a brighter future free from the destructive impact of compulsive gambling. Whether you are personally struggling with gambling addiction or supporting someone who is, know that help is available and recovery is possible. Let us take the next step forward on this journey towards healing and recovery.

Chapter 6: Building a Support System

Building a support system is a critical aspect of overcoming gambling addiction. Recovery is challenging, and having a robust network of supportive family, friends, and professionals can significantly enhance the chances of success. This chapter explores the importance of involving family and friends, the role of support groups and therapy, and the steps to create a safe and understanding environment conducive to recovery.

Involving Family and Friends

FAMILY AND FRIENDS play a pivotal role in the recovery journey. Their support, understanding, and involvement can provide the emotional and practical assistance needed to navigate the challenges of addiction recovery.

1. Understanding the Impact on Relationships:

Gambling addiction often strains relationships, leading to mistrust, resentment, and emotional distance. It's essential to acknowledge the impact that addiction has had on relationships and take steps to rebuild trust and communication.

- Open Communication: Open and honest communication is the foundation of rebuilding relationships. It's crucial to discuss the addiction openly, share feelings, and listen to each other's perspectives without judgment. This transparency helps create a sense of understanding and mutual support.

- Acknowledging Hurt and Pain: Both the individual struggling with addiction and their loved ones may have experienced hurt and pain. Acknowledging these feelings and validating each other's experiences can foster healing and empathy.

- Rebuilding Trust: Trust is often damaged by the secrecy and deceit associated with gambling addiction. Rebuilding trust takes time and consistent effort. Honesty, reliability, and transparency in actions are key to restoring trust in relationships.

2. Educating Loved Ones:

Educating family and friends about gambling addiction can help them understand the nature of the disorder and provide informed support. Knowledge about addiction can reduce stigma, promote empathy, and enhance the effectiveness of their support.

- Understanding Addiction: Providing loved ones with information about gambling addiction, its causes, and its effects can help them recognize that it is a complex disorder, not a moral failing. This understanding can shift their perspective and foster a more supportive attitude.

- Recognizing Triggers and Behaviors: Educating loved ones about the triggers and behaviors associated with gambling addiction can help them identify signs of relapse and offer timely support. This knowledge can also guide them in avoiding actions that might inadvertently enable the addiction.

- Accessing Resources: Sharing resources, such as books, articles, and support group information, can help loved ones learn more about gambling addiction and how to provide effective support. Encouraging them to attend educational workshops or therapy sessions can also be beneficial.

3. Providing Emotional Support:

Emotional support from family and friends is crucial for individuals in recovery. Knowing that they are not alone and that their loved ones believe in their ability to recover can provide motivation and strength.

- Empathy and Compassion: Showing empathy and compassion involves understanding the individual's struggles and offering non-judgmental support. This can help reduce feelings of shame and guilt and encourage open communication.

- Encouragement and Positivity: Providing encouragement and positive reinforcement can boost the individual's confidence and motivation. Celebrating small milestones and progress can reinforce their efforts and commitment to recovery.

- Patience and Understanding: Recovery is a gradual process, and setbacks are common. Patience and understanding from loved ones are essential in maintaining a supportive environment. Recognizing that relapse is a part of recovery and offering continued support can help individuals stay on track.

4. Practical Support:

Practical support can make a significant difference in the recovery process. Family and friends can assist with day-to-day responsibilities, financial management, and creating a structured environment that supports recovery.

- Assisting with Daily Responsibilities: Helping with daily tasks, such as household chores, childcare, or transportation, can reduce stress and allow the individual to focus on their recovery. This practical support can alleviate some of the pressures that might trigger a relapse.

- Financial Management: Offering assistance with financial management, such as creating a budget, managing debt, and setting up automatic bill payments, can help the individual regain financial stability. This support can reduce financial stress and prevent impulsive gambling behavior.

- Creating a Structured Environment: A structured environment can provide stability and reduce opportunities for gambling. Family and friends can help establish routines, set boundaries, and create a safe space that supports recovery efforts.

Support Groups and Therapy Options

SUPPORT GROUPS AND therapy are integral components of a comprehensive support system. They provide professional guidance, peer support, and structured approaches to addressing gambling addiction.

1. Support Groups:

Support groups offer a community of individuals who understand the challenges of gambling addiction. They provide a safe space to share experiences, receive support, and find accountability.

- Gamblers Anonymous (GA): GA is a well-known 12-step program specifically designed for individuals struggling with gambling addiction. The program involves attending regular meetings, working through the 12 steps, and receiving support from a sponsor and fellow members. The sense of community and shared experience in GA can be incredibly empowering.

- SMART Recovery: SMART Recovery offers an alternative to the 12-step approach, focusing on self-empowerment and self-reliance. The program provides tools and techniques based on cognitive-behavioral therapy (CBT) to help individuals manage their addiction. Meetings and online resources offer support and guidance for recovery.

- Online Support Groups: Online support groups and forums provide a convenient and accessible way to connect with others facing similar challenges. These platforms offer anonymity and flexibility, making it easier for individuals to seek support regardless of their location or schedule.

2. Therapy Options:

Professional therapy is a cornerstone of effective treatment for gambling addiction. Therapists trained in addiction treatment can help individuals explore the underlying causes of their behavior, develop coping strategies, and work towards recovery.

- Cognitive-Behavioral Therapy (CBT): CBT is one of the most effective therapeutic approaches for gambling addiction. It focuses on identifying and challenging distorted thoughts and beliefs related to gambling. CBT helps individuals develop healthier thinking patterns and coping mechanisms, reducing the compulsion to gamble.

- Motivational Interviewing (MI): MI is a therapeutic approach that helps individuals resolve ambivalence about change. It involves exploring the individual's motivations for change and enhancing their commitment to recovery. MI is particularly effective in increasing readiness to seek help and engage in treatment.

- Psychodynamic Therapy: Psychodynamic therapy explores the underlying emotional and psychological factors that contribute to gambling addiction. This approach helps individuals gain insight into their behavior and address unresolved issues, promoting long-term recovery.

- Family Therapy: Family therapy can be beneficial for addressing the impact of gambling addiction on relationships and family dynamics. It involves working with family members to improve communication, rebuild trust, and develop a supportive environment for recovery.

- Group Therapy: Group therapy provides a supportive and therapeutic environment where individuals can share their experiences and learn from others. The group dynamic offers different perspectives and collective wisdom, which can enhance the recovery process.

3. Integrating Support Groups and Therapy:

Integrating support groups and therapy can provide a comprehensive approach to recovery. Support groups offer peer support and a sense of community, while therapy provides professional guidance and personalized treatment.

- Complementary Benefits: Support groups and therapy can complement each other by addressing different aspects of recovery. Support groups provide ongoing peer support and accountability, while therapy offers individualized treatment and coping strategies.

- Consistent Participation: Regular participation in both support groups and therapy sessions can help individuals stay engaged and committed to their recovery. The combined support from peers and professionals can enhance resilience and reduce the risk of relapse.

- Building a Recovery Network: Engaging in multiple support systems can create a robust recovery network. This network provides diverse resources, perspectives, and support, increasing the chances of successful recovery.

Creating a Safe and Understanding Environment

CREATING A SAFE AND understanding environment is essential for supporting recovery from gambling addiction. This environment should be conducive to healing, promote positive behavior, and reduce triggers and stressors that could lead to relapse.

1. Establishing Boundaries and Routines:

Establishing clear boundaries and routines can provide structure and stability, reducing the likelihood of impulsive gambling behavior.

- Setting Clear Boundaries: Clear boundaries help define acceptable and unacceptable behaviors. This includes setting limits on financial spending, time spent on gambling-related activities, and interactions with individuals or environments that may trigger gambling.

- Creating Routines: Structured routines provide a sense of predictability and control. Establishing daily routines for work, leisure, and self-care can reduce stress and create a balanced lifestyle. Consistency in routines can also promote positive habits and behaviors.

2. Reducing Triggers and Temptations:

Identifying and reducing triggers and temptations is crucial for maintaining a safe environment. Triggers can include specific situations, emotions, or people that prompt the urge to gamble.

- Identifying Triggers: Recognizing the triggers that lead to gambling can help individuals and their loved ones develop strategies to avoid or manage them. Triggers can vary widely and may include stress, boredom, loneliness, or exposure to gambling environments.

- Creating a Trigger-Free Environment: Reducing exposure to gambling-related triggers can help prevent relapse. This may involve avoiding casinos, limiting access to online gambling sites, and removing gambling paraphernalia from the home.

- Developing Coping Strategies: Developing healthy coping strategies for managing triggers and cravings is essential. This can include engaging in alternative activities, practicing relaxation techniques, or seeking support from loved ones or support groups.

3. Promoting Positive Activities and Interests:

Encouraging and supporting positive activities and interests can provide fulfillment and reduce the urge to gamble. Engaging in new interests and hobbies can contribute to a sense of purpose and satisfaction.

- Exploring New Hobbies: Encouraging individuals to explore new hobbies and interests can provide a productive and enjoyable way to spend time. Creative activities, physical exercise, and social interactions can offer a sense of accomplishment and enjoyment.

- Supporting Personal Goals: Supporting individuals in setting and pursuing personal goals can provide motivation and direction. This might include career aspirations, educational pursuits, or personal development goals.

FOSTERING SOCIAL CONNECTIONS: Building and maintaining social connections can reduce feelings of isolation and provide emotional support. Encouraging participation in social activities, community events, and support groups can enhance overall well-being.

4. Encouraging Self-Care and Wellness:

Promoting self-care and wellness is crucial for supporting recovery. A focus on physical, emotional, and mental health can enhance resilience and overall quality of life.

- Physical Health: Encouraging regular physical exercise, a balanced diet, and adequate sleep can support physical health and reduce stress. Physical well-being is closely linked to emotional and mental health, contributing to overall resilience.

- Emotional Health: Supporting emotional health involves developing healthy coping mechanisms, practicing mindfulness, and seeking professional support when needed. Emotional well-being is essential for managing stress and reducing the risk of relapse.

- Mental Health: Prioritizing mental health involves addressing underlying psychological issues, such as anxiety, depression, or trauma. Seeking therapy and participating in support groups can provide the necessary support for mental health.

5. Celebrating Progress and Achievements:

Recognizing and celebrating progress and achievements can provide motivation and reinforce positive behavior. Celebrating milestones, no matter how small, can boost confidence and commitment to recovery.

- Acknowledging Milestones: Acknowledging milestones, such as a certain period of abstinence, attending therapy sessions, or achieving personal goals, can provide a sense of accomplishment. Celebrating these achievements can reinforce positive behavior and encourage continued progress.

- Positive Reinforcement: Providing positive reinforcement, such as praise, encouragement, or rewards, can motivate individuals to stay committed to their recovery. Positive reinforcement helps build self-esteem and confidence.

- Reflecting on Progress: Reflecting on the progress made during the recovery journey can provide perspective and motivation. Journaling, discussing achievements with loved ones, or participating in support group meetings can help individuals recognize their growth and resilience.

Moving Forward

BUILDING A SUPPORT system is a critical component of recovery from gambling addiction. Involving family and friends, participating in support groups and therapy, and creating a safe and understanding environment are essential steps in this process.

Family and friends play a vital role in providing emotional and practical support. Their understanding, encouragement, and involvement can significantly enhance the chances of successful recovery. Educating loved ones about gambling addiction, fostering open communication, and rebuilding trust are crucial for creating a supportive environment.

Support groups and therapy offer professional guidance and peer support. Integrating these resources can provide a comprehensive approach to recovery, addressing the psychological, emotional, and behavioral aspects of addiction. Regular participation in support groups and therapy can help individuals stay engaged and committed to their recovery.

Creating a safe and understanding environment involves establishing boundaries and routines, reducing triggers and temptations, promoting positive activities, and encouraging self-care and wellness. This environment should support healing, promote positive behavior, and reduce stressors that could lead to relapse.

As we continue to explore the various aspects of gambling addiction in this book, we will provide practical strategies and insights to support individuals on their path to recovery. Understanding the importance of building a support system is a crucial step in this process, as it equips individuals with the knowledge and tools needed to overcome addiction and rebuild their lives.

Together, we can build a brighter future free from the destructive impact of compulsive gambling. Whether you are personally struggling with gambling addiction or supporting someone who is, know that help is available and recovery is possible. Let us take the next step forward on this journey towards healing and recovery.

Chapter 7: Financial Recovery and Management

———

Financial recovery is a crucial component of overcoming gambling addiction. The financial damage caused by compulsive gambling can be severe, affecting not only the individual but also their family and loved ones. This chapter explores how to assess the financial damage, develop a recovery plan, and budget and manage money wisely to regain financial stability and security.

Assessing the Financial Damage

THE FIRST STEP IN FINANCIAL recovery is to assess the extent of the financial damage caused by gambling. This process can be daunting, but it is essential for developing a realistic and effective recovery plan.

1. Evaluating Debts and Liabilities:

Start by listing all outstanding debts and liabilities. This includes credit card debt, personal loans, payday loans, and any money borrowed from family and friends. Be thorough and honest in your assessment to get a clear picture of your financial situation.

- Credit Card Debt: Review all credit card statements to determine the total amount owed. Note the interest rates and minimum payments required for each card.

- Personal Loans: List all personal loans, including the outstanding balances, interest rates, and monthly payments.

- Payday Loans: Payday loans often come with high-interest rates and short repayment terms. Calculate the total amount owed, including any accrued interest and fees.

- Family and Friends: If you have borrowed money from family or friends, include these amounts in your assessment. Be clear about the terms of repayment, if any were agreed upon.

2. Reviewing Bank Statements and Transactions:

Review your bank statements and transactions for the past year to identify all gambling-related expenses. This includes money spent on online gambling, casino visits, lottery tickets, and any other gambling activities. Categorize these expenses to understand the total financial impact of your gambling behavior.

- Online Gambling: Sum up all transactions related to online gambling sites, including deposits and withdrawals.

- Casino Visits: Calculate the total amount spent on casino visits, including entry fees, chips purchased, and any additional expenses.

- Lottery Tickets: Add up the total amount spent on lottery tickets and other similar gambling activities.

3. Analyzing Income and Expenses:

Analyze your monthly income and expenses to identify any discrepancies or areas of concern. This will help you understand your cash flow and identify opportunities for improvement.

- Monthly Income: Calculate your total monthly income from all sources, including salary, bonuses, and any other sources of income.

- Monthly Expenses: List all monthly expenses, including rent or mortgage payments, utilities, groceries, transportation, insurance, and any other recurring costs.

- Discretionary Spending: Identify discretionary spending, such as dining out, entertainment, and non-essential purchases. This will help you identify areas where you can cut back to save money.

4. Identifying Assets and Savings:

List all assets and savings to understand your financial position. This includes cash savings, investments, retirement accounts, real estate, and any other valuable assets.

- Cash Savings: Calculate the total amount in your savings accounts and emergency fund.

- Investments: Review your investment portfolio, including stocks, bonds, mutual funds, and any other investment vehicles.

- Retirement Accounts: Note the balances in your retirement accounts, such as 401(k) or IRA.

- Real Estate: Assess the value of any real estate properties you own, including your primary residence and any investment properties.

- Valuable Assets: List any other valuable assets, such as vehicles, jewelry, or collectibles.

5. Understanding Credit Score and History:

Check your credit score and review your credit report to understand the impact of gambling on your credit history. Your credit score is an important factor in your financial health and can affect your ability to secure loans, rent housing, or obtain employment.

- Credit Score: Use a reputable credit monitoring service to check your credit score. Note any changes or discrepancies.

- Credit Report: Obtain a copy of your credit report from the major credit bureaus (Experian, Equifax, and TransUnion). Review the report for any errors or negative marks related to gambling.

Developing a Recovery Plan

ONCE YOU HAVE ASSESSED the financial damage, the next step is to develop a recovery plan. A well-structured plan will help you manage your debts, rebuild your finances, and achieve long-term financial stability.

1. Setting Financial Goals:

Set clear and realistic financial goals to guide your recovery plan. These goals should be specific, measurable, achievable, relevant, and time-bound (SMART).

- Short-Term Goals: Short-term goals focus on immediate financial needs, such as paying off high-interest debt, creating a budget, and building an emergency fund.

- Long-Term Goals: Long-term goals focus on future financial stability, such as saving for retirement, buying a home, or funding education.

2. Prioritizing Debt Repayment:

Prioritize your debts based on interest rates and repayment terms. Focus on paying off high-interest debt first to reduce the overall cost of your debt.

- High-Interest Debt: Pay off high-interest debt, such as credit card debt and payday loans, as quickly as possible. Consider using the debt avalanche method (paying off the highest interest rate debt first) or the debt snowball method (paying off the smallest debt first) to stay motivated.

- Debt Consolidation: If you have multiple high-interest debts, consider consolidating them into a single loan with a lower interest rate. This can simplify your payments and reduce the overall interest paid.

- Negotiating with Creditors: Contact your creditors to negotiate lower interest rates, reduced payments, or extended repayment terms. Many creditors are willing to work with you if you demonstrate a commitment to repaying your debt.

3. Creating a Budget:

A budget is a crucial tool for managing your money and staying on track with your financial goals. It helps you allocate your income, control your spending, and save for the future.

- Income Allocation: Allocate your income to cover essential expenses, debt repayment, savings, and discretionary spending. Use the 50/30/20 rule as a guideline: 50% for needs, 30% for wants, and 20% for savings and debt repayment.

- Expense Tracking: Track your expenses to ensure you stay within your budget. Use budgeting tools or apps to simplify this process and monitor your spending in real-time.

- Adjusting Your Budget: Regularly review and adjust your budget based on changes in your income, expenses, and financial goals. Be flexible and willing to make adjustments as needed.

4. Building an Emergency Fund:

An emergency fund is a critical component of financial stability. It provides a safety net for unexpected expenses and reduces the need to rely on credit or loans.

- Saving for Emergencies: Aim to save at least three to six months' worth of living expenses in your emergency fund. Start by setting aside a small amount each month and gradually increase your contributions as your financial situation improves.

- Accessibility: Keep your emergency fund in a separate, easily accessible account, such as a high-yield savings account. This ensures you can access the funds quickly when needed.

5. Rebuilding Credit:

Rebuilding your credit is an essential step in financial recovery. A good credit score opens doors to better financial opportunities and lower interest rates.

- Timely Payments: Make all debt payments on time to avoid late fees and negative marks on your credit report. Set up automatic payments or reminders to ensure you never miss a payment.

- Credit Utilization: Keep your credit utilization ratio (the amount of credit you're using compared to your total credit limit) below 30%. This demonstrates responsible credit management and positively impacts your credit score.

- Secured Credit Cards: If your credit score is low, consider using a secured credit card to rebuild your credit. Secured credit cards require a security deposit, which acts as collateral and sets your credit limit. Use the card responsibly and pay off the balance in full each month to improve your credit score.

- Credit Monitoring: Regularly monitor your credit report and score to track your progress and identify any errors or discrepancies. Dispute any inaccuracies with the credit bureaus to ensure your report is accurate.

6. Seeking Professional Help:

Professional help can provide valuable guidance and support during your financial recovery. Financial advisors, credit counselors, and therapists can offer expert advice and strategies to help you achieve your goals.

- Financial Advisors: A financial advisor can help you develop a comprehensive financial plan, manage your investments, and provide guidance on complex financial matters. Choose an advisor with experience in dealing with gambling addiction and financial recovery.

- Credit Counselors: Credit counselors can assist with budgeting, debt management, and credit repair. They can also help negotiate with creditors and develop a debt repayment plan. Look for certified credit counselors through reputable organizations, such as the National Foundation for Credit Counseling (NFCC).

- Therapists: A therapist with experience in addiction recovery can help you address the psychological and emotional aspects of gambling addiction. Therapy can provide tools and coping strategies to manage triggers, reduce cravings, and support long-term recovery.

Budgeting and Managing Money Wisely

EFFECTIVE BUDGETING and money management are key to maintaining financial stability and preventing relapse into gambling behavior. Developing healthy financial habits can support your recovery and help you achieve your financial goals.

1. Understanding Your Spending Habits:

Understanding your spending habits is the first step in creating a budget and managing your money wisely. Analyze your spending patterns to identify areas where you can cut back and save.

- Tracking Expenses: Track all your expenses for at least one month to get a clear picture of your spending habits. Categorize your expenses into essential (needs) and non-essential (wants) to identify areas for improvement.

- Identifying Patterns: Look for patterns in your spending, such as frequent dining out, impulse purchases, or entertainment expenses. Recognizing these patterns can help you make informed decisions about where to cut back.

2. Creating a Realistic Budget:

A realistic budget reflects your income, expenses, and financial goals. It helps you allocate your resources effectively and stay on track with your financial plan.

- Fixed vs. Variable Expenses: Separate your fixed expenses (e.g., rent, utilities, loan payments) from your variable expenses (e.g., groceries, entertainment, discretionary spending). This distinction helps you prioritize essential costs and manage fluctuating expenses.

- Setting Spending Limits: Set spending limits for each category in your budget. Be realistic about your needs and wants, and allocate funds accordingly. Ensure that your budget allows for savings and debt repayment.

- Using Budgeting Tools: Use budgeting tools or apps to simplify the budgeting process and track your progress. Tools like Mint, YNAB (You Need a Budget), or personal finance spreadsheets can help you stay organized and monitor your spending.

3. Implementing the Envelope System:

The envelope system is a practical budgeting method that involves allocating cash for different spending categories. This system helps you control your spending and avoid overspending.

- Categorizing Expenses: Divide your expenses into categories, such as groceries, entertainment, dining out, and discretionary spending. Allocate a specific amount of cash to each category based on your budget.

- Using Envelopes: Place the allocated cash into labeled envelopes for each spending category. Use only the cash in each envelope for the designated expenses. When the cash is gone, stop spending in that category until the next budget period.

- Tracking Spending: Keep track of your spending by recording each transaction on the envelope. This helps you stay accountable and monitor your spending habits.

4. Building an Emergency Fund:

An emergency fund is essential for financial stability. It provides a safety net for unexpected expenses and reduces the need to rely on credit or loans.

- Setting Savings Goals: Set a goal to save at least three to six months' worth of living expenses in your emergency fund. Start by saving a small amount each month and gradually increase your contributions as your financial situation improves.

- Automating Savings: Automate your savings by setting up automatic transfers from your checking account to your savings account. This ensures consistent contributions and makes saving a priority.

- Choosing the Right Account: Keep your emergency fund in a separate, easily accessible account, such as a high-yield savings account. This ensures you can access the funds quickly when needed.

5. Reducing Debt:

Reducing debt is a critical component of financial recovery. Focus on paying off high-interest debt first to reduce the overall cost of your debt.

- Debt Repayment Strategies: Consider using the debt avalanche method (paying off the highest interest rate debt first) or the debt snowball method (paying off the smallest debt first) to stay motivated. Both strategies can help you reduce your debt and achieve financial freedom.

- Debt Consolidation: If you have multiple high-interest debts, consider consolidating them into a single loan with a lower interest rate. This can simplify your payments and reduce the overall interest paid.

- Negotiating with Creditors: Contact your creditors to negotiate lower interest rates, reduced payments, or extended repayment terms. Many creditors are willing to work with you if you demonstrate a commitment to repaying your debt.

6. Avoiding Impulse Purchases:

Impulse purchases can derail your budget and lead to unnecessary spending. Developing strategies to avoid impulsive buying can help you stay on track with your financial goals.

- Creating a Shopping List: Make a shopping list before you go shopping and stick to it. This helps you avoid impulse purchases and focus on buying only what you need.

- Implementing a Waiting Period: Implement a waiting period for non-essential purchases. Wait at least 24 hours before making a purchase to determine if it is a necessary and thoughtful decision.

- Avoiding Temptation: Avoid situations that may trigger impulsive buying, such as browsing online stores or visiting shopping malls without a specific purpose. Unsubscribe from marketing emails and remove shopping apps from your phone to reduce temptation.

7. Building Healthy Financial Habits:

Developing healthy financial habits is essential for maintaining financial stability and achieving long-term goals. These habits can help you manage your money wisely and prevent relapse into gambling behavior.

- Saving Regularly: Make saving a regular habit by setting aside a portion of your income each month. Treat savings as a non-negotiable expense and prioritize it in your budget.

- Reviewing Your Budget: Regularly review and adjust your budget based on changes in your income, expenses, and financial goals. Be flexible and willing to make adjustments as needed.

- Seeking Financial Education: Continuously seek financial education to improve your money management skills. Read books, attend workshops, and use online resources to stay informed about personal finance.

8. Seeking Professional Help:

Professional help can provide valuable guidance and support during your financial recovery. Financial advisors, credit counselors, and therapists can offer expert advice and strategies to help you achieve your goals.

- Financial Advisors: A financial advisor can help you develop a comprehensive financial plan, manage your investments, and provide guidance on complex financial matters. Choose an advisor with experience in dealing with gambling addiction and financial recovery.

- Credit Counselors: Credit counselors can assist with budgeting, debt management, and credit repair. They can also help negotiate with creditors and develop a debt repayment plan. Look for certified credit counselors through reputable organizations, such as the National Foundation for Credit Counseling (NFCC).

- Therapists: A therapist with experience in addiction recovery can help you address the psychological and emotional aspects of gambling addiction. Therapy can provide tools and coping strategies to manage triggers, reduce cravings, and support long-term recovery.

Moving Forward

FINANCIAL RECOVERY and management are critical components of overcoming gambling addiction. Assessing the financial damage, developing a recovery plan, and budgeting and managing money wisely are essential steps in this process.

Assessing the financial damage involves evaluating debts and liabilities, reviewing bank statements and transactions, analyzing income and expenses, identifying assets and savings, and understanding credit score and history. This comprehensive assessment provides a clear picture of your financial situation and guides the development of a recovery plan.

Developing a recovery plan includes setting financial goals, prioritizing debt repayment, creating a budget, building an emergency fund, rebuilding credit, and seeking professional help. A well-structured recovery plan provides a roadmap to financial stability and long-term success.

Budgeting and managing money wisely involve understanding spending habits, creating a realistic budget, implementing the envelope system, building an emergency fund, reducing debt, avoiding impulse purchases, building healthy financial habits, and seeking professional help. These strategies support financial stability and help prevent relapse into gambling behavior.

As we continue to explore the various aspects of gambling addiction in this book, we will provide practical strategies and insights to support individuals on their path to recovery. Understanding the importance of financial recovery and management is a crucial step in this process, as it equips individuals with the knowledge and tools needed to overcome addiction and rebuild their lives.

Together, we can build a brighter future free from the destructive impact of compulsive gambling. Whether you are personally struggling with gambling addiction or supporting someone who is, know that help is available and recovery is possible. Let us take the next step forward on this journey towards healing and recovery.

Chapter 8: Developing Healthy Habits

Developing healthy habits is a cornerstone of recovery from gambling addiction. Positive activities, new hobbies, and a focus on physical and mental well-being can fill the void left by gambling and contribute to a balanced, fulfilling life. This chapter will explore how to replace gambling with positive activities, build new hobbies and interests, and prioritize physical and mental health to support long-term recovery.

Replacing Gambling with Positive Activities

REPLACING GAMBLING with positive activities is essential for breaking the cycle of addiction. These activities can provide a sense of purpose, fulfillment, and enjoyment without the harmful consequences associated with gambling.

1. Identifying Triggers and Developing Alternatives:

Understanding the triggers that lead to gambling can help in developing effective alternatives. Common triggers include boredom, stress, loneliness, and the need for excitement. Identifying these triggers allows for the creation of personalized strategies to manage them.

- Stress Management: Engage in activities that reduce stress, such as meditation, yoga, deep breathing exercises, or progressive muscle relaxation. These practices can help calm the mind and body, making it easier to cope with stress without turning to gambling.

- Social Interaction: Combat loneliness by connecting with friends and family, joining clubs or groups, or participating in community events. Building a strong social network can provide support and reduce the urge to gamble.

- Productive Engagement: Replace boredom with productive activities that stimulate the mind and body. Consider learning new skills, volunteering, or pursuing educational opportunities.

2. Setting Realistic Goals:

Setting realistic and achievable goals can provide motivation and a sense of direction. Goals give structure to daily life and create a sense of accomplishment when achieved.

- Short-Term Goals: Short-term goals are immediate and manageable, such as exercising three times a week, attending a support group meeting, or completing a project. These goals can provide quick wins and boost confidence.

- Long-Term Goals: Long-term goals focus on broader aspirations, such as career advancement, financial stability, or personal growth. These goals require sustained effort and provide a roadmap for future success.

3. Engaging in Physical Activities:

Physical activities offer numerous benefits, including improved physical health, reduced stress, and enhanced mood. Regular exercise can also provide a healthy outlet for energy and emotions.

- Cardiovascular Exercise: Activities such as running, swimming, cycling, or aerobics can improve cardiovascular health, increase stamina, and boost mood through the release of endorphins.

- Strength Training: Strength training exercises, such as weightlifting, resistance band workouts, or bodyweight exercises, can build muscle, improve bone density, and enhance overall fitness.

- Outdoor Activities: Engaging in outdoor activities, such as hiking, gardening, or playing sports, can provide fresh air, sunlight, and a connection to nature, all of which contribute to well-being.

4. Exploring Creative Outlets:

Creative activities can provide an enjoyable and fulfilling way to express oneself and explore new interests. These outlets can also serve as a form of therapy, helping to process emotions and reduce stress.

- Art: Drawing, painting, sculpting, or other forms of visual art can provide a creative and therapeutic outlet. Art classes or workshops can offer guidance and a sense of community.

- Music: Playing a musical instrument, singing, or composing music can be both relaxing and stimulating. Joining a choir, band, or music group can also provide social interaction and a sense of belonging.

- Writing: Writing, whether through journaling, poetry, or creative writing, can help process emotions and clarify thoughts. Writing workshops or groups can offer support and feedback.

5. Volunteering and Giving Back:

Volunteering and giving back to the community can provide a sense of purpose and fulfillment. Helping others can also shift focus away from personal struggles and promote a sense of connection and empathy.

- Community Service: Volunteering at local organizations, such as food banks, shelters, or community centers, can provide meaningful engagement and make a positive impact.

- Mentorship: Becoming a mentor to someone in need, such as a student or a person struggling with similar challenges, can offer valuable support and foster personal growth.

- Charitable Activities: Participating in charitable activities, such as fundraising events, charity runs, or donation drives, can contribute to a greater cause and promote a sense of altruism.

Building New Hobbies and Interests

BUILDING NEW HOBBIES and interests is essential for creating a fulfilling and balanced life. These activities can provide enjoyment, personal growth, and a sense of accomplishment.

1. Exploring New Interests:

Exploring new interests can open up a world of possibilities and provide fresh excitement and engagement.

- Trying New Activities: Be open to trying new activities and stepping out of your comfort zone. Attend workshops, classes, or events that introduce new hobbies and interests.

- Learning and Education: Pursue educational opportunities to expand knowledge and skills. This can include enrolling in courses, attending seminars, or participating in online learning platforms.

- Travel and Exploration: Traveling to new places and experiencing different cultures can broaden perspectives and provide new experiences. Even local exploration, such as visiting museums, parks, or historical sites, can be enriching.

2. Developing Skills and Talents:

Developing skills and talents can provide a sense of accomplishment and boost self-esteem. Pursuing interests that align with natural abilities can lead to mastery and personal fulfillment.

- Artistic Skills: Develop artistic skills through practice and instruction. Whether it's painting, drawing, photography, or another form of art, honing these skills can be deeply satisfying.

- Technical Skills: Learn technical skills, such as coding, graphic design, or woodworking. These skills can lead to new career opportunities or personal projects.

- Culinary Skills: Exploring culinary skills through cooking and baking can be both enjoyable and practical. Experimenting with new recipes, techniques, and cuisines can provide a creative outlet and enhance daily life.

3. Participating in Group Activities:

Group activities provide social interaction, support, and a sense of community. Engaging with others who share similar interests can enhance enjoyment and foster connections.

- Sports Teams: Joining a sports team or recreational league can provide physical exercise, teamwork, and camaraderie. Whether it's soccer, basketball, or tennis, participating in sports can be a great way to stay active and connected.

- Clubs and Organizations: Joining clubs or organizations that align with your interests can provide a sense of belonging and opportunities for engagement. This can include book clubs, gardening clubs, or hobbyist groups.

- Workshops and Classes: Attend workshops and classes to learn new skills and meet like-minded individuals. Many community centers, libraries, and educational institutions offer a variety of classes and events.

4. Pursuing Personal Growth:

Personal growth activities focus on self-improvement, self-awareness, and the development of a positive mindset.

- Mindfulness and Meditation: Practicing mindfulness and meditation can enhance self-awareness, reduce stress, and promote emotional well-being. Guided meditation apps or classes can provide structure and support.

- Self-Help and Personal Development: Reading self-help books, attending seminars, or participating in personal development programs can provide valuable insights and tools for growth.

- Goal Setting and Achievement: Set personal goals that align with your values and aspirations. Break these goals into manageable steps and celebrate achievements along the way.

Focusing on Physical and Mental Well-Being

FOCUSING ON PHYSICAL and mental well-being is essential for overall health and long-term recovery. Prioritizing self-care, maintaining a healthy lifestyle, and seeking professional support can enhance resilience and well-being.

1. Physical Health:

Maintaining physical health through regular exercise, proper nutrition, and adequate sleep is crucial for overall well-being.

- Regular Exercise: Engage in regular physical activity that you enjoy. This can include cardiovascular exercise, strength training, or recreational sports. Aim for at least 150 minutes of moderate-intensity exercise per week.

- Balanced Diet: Eat a balanced diet that includes a variety of nutrients. Focus on whole foods, such as fruits, vegetables, lean proteins, whole grains, and healthy fats. Avoid excessive consumption of processed foods, sugar, and alcohol.

- Adequate Sleep: Prioritize getting enough sleep each night. Aim for 7-9 hours of sleep per night and establish a consistent sleep routine. Create a relaxing bedtime environment and avoid screens before bedtime.

2. Mental Health:

Maintaining mental health through stress management, emotional regulation, and professional support is essential for overall well-being.

- Stress Management: Practice stress management techniques, such as mindfulness, deep breathing exercises, or progressive muscle relaxation. These practices can help calm the mind and body, making it easier to cope with stress.

- Emotional Regulation: Develop healthy coping mechanisms for managing emotions. This can include journaling, talking to a trusted friend or therapist, or engaging in creative outlets.

- Professional Support: Seek professional support if needed. A therapist or counselor can provide valuable tools and coping strategies to manage mental health challenges and support long-term recovery.

3. Social Connections:

Building and maintaining social connections can reduce feelings of isolation and provide emotional support.

- Building a Support Network: Surround yourself with supportive and understanding individuals. This can include family, friends, support groups, or community organizations.

- Nurturing Relationships: Invest time and effort in nurturing relationships. Communicate openly, show empathy, and be present for your loved ones.

- Participating in Social Activities: Engage in social activities that bring joy and connection. This can include attending events, joining clubs, or participating in group activities.

4. Practicing Self-Care:

Self-care involves taking intentional actions to care for your physical, mental, and emotional well-being.

- Mindful Activities: Engage in activities that promote mindfulness and relaxation. This can include meditation, yoga, or spending time in nature.

- Relaxation Techniques: Practice relaxation techniques, such as deep breathing exercises, progressive muscle relaxation, or guided imagery. These techniques can help reduce stress and promote a sense of calm.

- Personal Enjoyment: Take time for activities that bring joy and fulfillment. This can include hobbies, creative outlets, or spending time with loved ones.

Building a Sustainable Recovery

BUILDING A SUSTAINABLE recovery involves integrating healthy habits into daily life and creating a supportive environment for long-term success.

1. Developing a Routine:

Developing a consistent daily routine can provide structure and stability, reducing the likelihood of relapse.

- Daily Schedule: Create a daily schedule that includes time for work, exercise, relaxation, social activities, and self-care. A consistent routine can help you stay organized and focused.

- Prioritizing Activities: Prioritize activities that support your recovery and well-being. Make time for positive activities, hobbies, and self-care.

- Flexibility: Be flexible and willing to adjust your routine as needed. Life is unpredictable, and being adaptable can help you manage changes and challenges.

2. Setting Boundaries:

Setting boundaries is essential for protecting your well-being and maintaining a healthy lifestyle.

- Personal Boundaries: Establish personal boundaries that protect your time, energy, and mental health. This can include setting limits on social interactions, work commitments, or recreational activities.

- Social Boundaries: Set boundaries with others to protect your recovery. This can include limiting contact with individuals who may trigger gambling behavior or avoiding environments that promote gambling.

- Self-Respect: Respect your own boundaries and be assertive in communicating them to others. Prioritize your well-being and recovery.

3. Seeking Continued Support:

Continued support is essential for long-term recovery. Engage with support groups, therapy, and loved ones to stay connected and motivated.

- Support Groups: Continue participating in support groups, such as Gamblers Anonymous or SMART Recovery. These groups provide ongoing peer support and accountability.

- Therapy: Maintain regular therapy sessions to address ongoing challenges and develop new coping strategies. Therapy can provide valuable insights and support for long-term recovery.

- Loved Ones: Stay connected with loved ones who support your recovery. Open communication and mutual understanding can strengthen relationships and provide emotional support.

4. Monitoring Progress:

Monitoring your progress can provide motivation and a sense of accomplishment. Regularly review your goals, achievements, and areas for improvement.

- Journaling: Keep a journal to track your progress, reflect on your experiences, and set new goals. Journaling can provide clarity and self-awareness.

- Celebrating Milestones: Celebrate milestones and achievements along your recovery journey. Recognize your efforts and reward yourself for your hard work.

- Adjusting Goals: Regularly review and adjust your goals based on your progress and changing circumstances. Be flexible and willing to adapt to new challenges and opportunities.

Moving Forward

DEVELOPING HEALTHY habits is a crucial component of recovery from gambling addiction. Replacing gambling with positive activities, building new hobbies and interests, and focusing on physical and mental well-being can provide a balanced and fulfilling life.

Replacing gambling with positive activities involves identifying triggers, setting realistic goals, engaging in physical activities, exploring creative outlets, and volunteering. These activities provide purpose, fulfillment, and enjoyment without the harmful consequences of gambling.

Building new hobbies and interests involves exploring new activities, developing skills and talents, participating in group activities, and pursuing personal growth. These hobbies provide engagement, personal growth, and a sense of accomplishment.

Focusing on physical and mental well-being involves maintaining physical health through exercise, nutrition, and sleep, maintaining mental health through stress management, emotional regulation, and professional support, building social connections, and practicing self-care. These practices enhance resilience and overall well-being.

Building a sustainable recovery involves developing a routine, setting boundaries, seeking continued support, and monitoring progress. These strategies provide structure, stability, and ongoing motivation for long-term success.

As we continue to explore the various aspects of gambling addiction in this book, we will provide practical strategies and insights to support individuals on their path to recovery. Understanding the importance of developing healthy habits is a crucial step in this process, as it equips individuals with the knowledge and tools needed to overcome addiction and rebuild their lives.

Together, we can build a brighter future free from the destructive impact of compulsive gambling. Whether you are personally struggling with gambling addiction or supporting someone who is, know that help is available and recovery is possible. Let us take the next step forward on this journey towards healing and recovery.

Chapter 9: Mindfulness and Stress Management

Stress and anxiety are common issues that can exacerbate gambling addiction and hinder recovery. Developing effective stress management techniques and practicing mindfulness can significantly improve mental and emotional well-being. This chapter explores various techniques for reducing stress and anxiety, the practice of mindfulness and meditation, and the benefits of maintaining a balanced lifestyle.

Techniques for Reducing Stress and Anxiety

STRESS AND ANXIETY can be overwhelming, but there are numerous techniques to manage these emotions effectively. Implementing these strategies can help create a more serene and controlled life, conducive to recovery and overall well-being.

1. Deep Breathing Exercises:

Deep breathing is a simple yet powerful technique for reducing stress and anxiety. It involves focusing on your breath and taking slow, deep breaths to calm the mind and body.

- Basic Deep Breathing: Sit or lie down in a comfortable position. Close your eyes and take a slow, deep breath in through your nose, allowing your abdomen to expand. Hold the breath for a few seconds, then slowly exhale through your mouth. Repeat this process for several minutes.

- 4-7-8 Breathing: This technique involves inhaling for a count of four, holding the breath for a count of seven, and exhaling for a count of eight. This longer exhalation helps to relax the nervous system and reduce anxiety.

- Diaphragmatic Breathing: Focus on breathing deeply into your diaphragm rather than shallowly into your chest. Place one hand on your chest and the other on your abdomen. Breathe deeply into your abdomen so that your lower hand rises, while your upper hand remains relatively still.

2. Progressive Muscle Relaxation (PMR):

PMR is a technique that involves tensing and then relaxing different muscle groups in the body. This practice helps to reduce physical tension and promote relaxation.

- How to Practice PMR: Begin by finding a quiet, comfortable place to sit or lie down. Starting with your toes, tense the muscles for about five seconds, then slowly release the tension. Move up through your body, tensing and relaxing each muscle group, including your legs, abdomen, arms, and face. Focus on the sensation of relaxation as you release each muscle group.

3. Visualization and Guided Imagery:

Visualization involves imagining a peaceful scene or situation to promote relaxation. Guided imagery is a similar technique that involves following a narrative or script that leads you through calming visualizations.

- How to Practice Visualization: Find a quiet place to sit or lie down comfortably. Close your eyes and imagine a serene place, such as a beach, forest, or mountain. Focus on the details of this place, including the sights, sounds, and smells. Allow yourself to become fully immersed in this peaceful environment.

- Guided Imagery Resources: Use guided imagery recordings or apps that provide calming narratives to lead you through relaxing visualizations. These resources can be found online or through meditation and wellness apps.

4. Physical Exercise:

Regular physical exercise is an effective way to reduce stress and anxiety. Exercise releases endorphins, which are natural mood lifters, and helps to reduce the levels of stress hormones in the body.

- Cardiovascular Exercise: Activities such as running, cycling, swimming, or brisk walking can increase heart rate and promote the release of endorphins. Aim for at least 150 minutes of moderate-intensity exercise per week.

- Strength Training: Incorporate strength training exercises, such as weightlifting or resistance band workouts, to build muscle and improve overall fitness. Strength training can also boost self-confidence and mental well-being.

- Mind-Body Exercises: Activities like yoga, tai chi, and Pilates combine physical movement with mindfulness and deep breathing, making them particularly effective for reducing stress and promoting relaxation.

5. Journaling and Expressive Writing:

Journaling and expressive writing can help process emotions and reduce stress by providing an outlet for thoughts and feelings.

- Daily Journaling: Set aside time each day to write about your experiences, thoughts, and emotions. This practice can help clarify your feelings, identify patterns, and release pent-up emotions.

- Gratitude Journaling: Focus on positive aspects of your life by keeping a gratitude journal. Each day, write down three things you are grateful for. This practice can shift your focus from stressors to positive experiences and promote a more optimistic outlook.

- Expressive Writing Prompts: Use prompts to guide your writing and explore specific emotions or experiences. Prompts such as "Describe a time when you felt overwhelmed and how you overcame it" or "Write about a place that makes you feel calm and why" can be helpful.

6. Social Support and Connection:

Maintaining strong social connections and seeking support from loved ones can significantly reduce stress and anxiety.

- Talking to Friends and Family: Share your thoughts and feelings with trusted friends or family members. Having someone to talk to can provide emotional support and reduce feelings of isolation.

- Joining Support Groups: Participate in support groups or therapy groups where you can connect with others who are experiencing similar challenges. These groups provide a sense of community and mutual understanding.

- Building New Connections: Engage in social activities and hobbies that interest you. Meeting new people and building new relationships can provide additional support and enjoyment.

7. Time Management and Organization:

Effective time management and organization can reduce stress by helping you prioritize tasks and manage responsibilities more efficiently.

- Creating a Schedule: Develop a daily or weekly schedule that includes time for work, self-care, social activities, and relaxation. A structured routine can provide a sense of control and reduce stress.

- Prioritizing Tasks: Identify and prioritize tasks based on their importance and urgency. Focus on completing high-priority tasks first and break larger tasks into smaller, manageable steps.

- Decluttering: Organize your physical environment by decluttering and creating a tidy, organized space. A clean and orderly environment can reduce stress and improve focus.

Practicing Mindfulness and Meditation

MINDFULNESS AND MEDITATION are powerful practices that can help reduce stress, improve mental clarity, and enhance overall well-being. These practices involve focusing on the present moment and cultivating a non-judgmental awareness of thoughts, feelings, and sensations.

1. Understanding Mindfulness:

Mindfulness is the practice of being fully present and engaged in the current moment. It involves paying attention to thoughts, feelings, and sensations without judgment or distraction.

- Benefits of Mindfulness: Mindfulness can reduce stress, improve emotional regulation, enhance concentration, and promote overall well-being. It can also help individuals develop greater self-awareness and resilience.

- Mindful Awareness: Practice bringing mindful awareness to everyday activities, such as eating, walking, or washing dishes. Focus on the sensations, movements, and thoughts that arise during these activities without judgment.

2. Basic Mindfulness Meditation:

Mindfulness meditation is a foundational practice that involves focusing on the breath and observing thoughts and sensations without attachment.

- How to Practice Mindfulness Meditation: Find a quiet place to sit comfortably. Close your eyes and bring your attention to your breath. Notice the sensation of the breath as it enters and leaves your nostrils or the rise and fall of your abdomen. If your mind wanders, gently bring your focus back to the breath without judgment. Practice for 5-10 minutes to start, gradually increasing the duration as you become more comfortable.

3. Body Scan Meditation:

Body scan meditation involves bringing mindful awareness to different parts of the body, promoting relaxation and a deeper connection to physical sensations.

- How to Practice Body Scan Meditation: Lie down or sit comfortably and close your eyes. Begin by bringing your attention to your toes and slowly move your focus up through your body, noticing any sensations, tension, or areas of relaxation. Spend a few moments on each part of the body before moving on. This practice can help release physical tension and promote relaxation.

4. Loving-Kindness Meditation (Metta):

Loving-kindness meditation involves cultivating feelings of compassion and kindness towards oneself and others. This practice can enhance emotional well-being and foster a sense of connection.

- How to Practice Loving-Kindness Meditation: Sit comfortably and close your eyes. Begin by directing loving-kindness towards yourself, silently repeating phrases such as "May I be happy, may I be healthy, may I be safe, may I live with ease." Gradually extend these feelings to others, including loved ones, acquaintances, and even those with whom you have conflicts. This practice can help cultivate a sense of compassion and interconnectedness.

5. Guided Meditation:

Guided meditation involves following a recorded or live narrative that leads you through a meditation practice. This can be helpful for beginners or those who prefer structured guidance.

- Using Guided Meditation Resources: Utilize guided meditation recordings, apps, or online resources that provide structured meditation sessions. These resources often include various themes, such as relaxation, stress reduction, or sleep support.

6. Mindful Movement:

Mindful movement practices, such as yoga, tai chi, and qigong, combine physical movement with mindful awareness and deep breathing.

- Yoga: Practice yoga to improve flexibility, strength, and relaxation. Focus on the breath and body sensations during each pose, bringing mindful awareness to the movements.

- Tai Chi and Qigong: Engage in tai chi or qigong, which involve slow, flowing movements coordinated with deep breathing. These practices promote relaxation, balance, and a sense of calm.

7. Incorporating Mindfulness into Daily Life:

Mindfulness can be integrated into daily activities to promote a sense of presence and reduce stress.

- Mindful Eating: Practice mindful eating by paying full attention to the experience of eating. Notice the colors, textures, and flavors of your food, and chew slowly and mindfully. This practice can enhance the enjoyment of meals and promote healthier eating habits.

- Mindful Walking: Engage in mindful walking by focusing on the sensations of walking, such as the movement of your legs

and the contact of your feet with the ground. Notice the sights, sounds, and smells around you, bringing your attention fully to the present moment.

- Mindful Listening: Practice mindful listening during conversations by giving your full attention to the speaker without interrupting or planning your response. This can enhance communication and foster deeper connections with others.

Benefits of a Balanced Lifestyle

MAINTAINING A BALANCED lifestyle is essential for overall well-being and long-term recovery from gambling addiction. A balanced lifestyle involves integrating physical health, mental well-being, social connections, and personal growth into daily life.

1. Physical Health:

Prioritizing physical health through regular exercise, proper nutrition, and adequate sleep can enhance energy levels, reduce stress, and improve overall well-being.

- Regular Exercise: Engage in regular physical activity that you enjoy. Aim for at least 150 minutes of moderate-intensity exercise per week. Exercise can improve cardiovascular health, boost mood, and reduce stress.

- Balanced Diet: Eat a balanced diet that includes a variety of nutrients. Focus on whole foods, such as fruits, vegetables, lean proteins, whole grains, and healthy fats. Avoid excessive consumption of processed foods, sugar, and alcohol.

- Adequate Sleep: Prioritize getting enough sleep each night. Aim for 7-9 hours of sleep per night and establish a consistent sleep routine. Create a relaxing bedtime environment and avoid screens before bedtime.

2. Mental Well-Being:

Maintaining mental well-being through stress management, emotional regulation, and professional support is essential for overall health and recovery.

- Stress Management: Practice stress management techniques, such as mindfulness, deep breathing exercises, or progressive muscle relaxation. These practices can help calm the mind and body, making it easier to cope with stress.

- Emotional Regulation: Develop healthy coping mechanisms for managing emotions. This can include journaling, talking to a trusted friend or therapist, or engaging in creative outlets.

- Professional Support: Seek professional support if needed. A therapist or counselor can provide valuable tools and coping strategies to manage mental health challenges and support long-term recovery.

3. Social Connections:

Building and maintaining social connections can reduce feelings of isolation and provide emotional support.

- Building a Support Network: Surround yourself with supportive and understanding individuals. This can include family, friends, support groups, or community organizations.

- Nurturing Relationships: Invest time and effort in nurturing relationships. Communicate openly, show empathy, and be present for your loved ones.

- Participating in Social Activities: Engage in social activities that bring joy and connection. This can include attending events, joining clubs, or participating in group activities.

4. Personal Growth:

Pursuing personal growth and self-improvement can enhance self-awareness, boost confidence, and provide a sense of purpose.

- Mindfulness and Meditation: Practice mindfulness and meditation to enhance self-awareness, reduce stress, and promote emotional well-being. Guided meditation apps or classes can provide structure and support.

- Self-Help and Personal Development: Read self-help books, attend seminars, or participate in personal development programs to gain valuable insights and tools for growth.

- Goal Setting and Achievement: Set personal goals that align with your values and aspirations. Break these goals into manageable steps and celebrate achievements along the way.

Integrating Mindfulness and Stress Management into Recovery

INTEGRATING MINDFULNESS and stress management techniques into your recovery journey can enhance resilience, reduce the risk of relapse, and support long-term success.

1. Developing a Routine:

Developing a consistent daily routine that includes mindfulness and stress management practices can provide structure and stability.

- Daily Mindfulness Practice: Incorporate a daily mindfulness practice, such as meditation or mindful breathing, into your routine. Even a few minutes each day can make a significant difference in reducing stress and enhancing well-being.

- Regular Exercise: Schedule regular exercise sessions to promote physical health and reduce stress. Choose activities that you enjoy and that fit into your lifestyle.

- Time for Self-Care: Set aside time each day for self-care activities that promote relaxation and well-being. This can include reading, taking a bath, or spending time in nature.

2. Setting Boundaries:

Setting boundaries is essential for protecting your well-being and maintaining a healthy lifestyle.

- Personal Boundaries: Establish personal boundaries that protect your time, energy, and mental health. This can include setting limits on social interactions, work commitments, or recreational activities.

- Social Boundaries: Set boundaries with others to protect your recovery. This can include limiting contact with individuals who may trigger gambling behavior or avoiding environments that promote gambling.

- Self-Respect: Respect your own boundaries and be assertive in communicating them to others. Prioritize your well-being and recovery.

3. Seeking Continued Support:

Continued support is essential for long-term recovery. Engage with support groups, therapy, and loved ones to stay connected and motivated.

- Support Groups: Continue participating in support groups, such as Gamblers Anonymous or SMART Recovery. These groups provide ongoing peer support and accountability.

- Therapy: Maintain regular therapy sessions to address ongoing challenges and develop new coping strategies. Therapy can provide valuable insights and support for long-term recovery.

- Loved Ones: Stay connected with loved ones who support your recovery. Open communication and mutual understanding can strengthen relationships and provide emotional support.

4. Monitoring Progress:

Monitoring your progress can provide motivation and a sense of accomplishment. Regularly review your goals, achievements, and areas for improvement.

- Journaling: Keep a journal to track your progress, reflect on your experiences, and set new goals. Journaling can provide clarity and self-awareness.

- Celebrating Milestones: Celebrate milestones and achievements along your recovery journey. Recognize your efforts and reward yourself for your hard work.

- Adjusting Goals: Regularly review and adjust your goals based on your progress and changing circumstances. Be flexible and willing to adapt to new challenges and opportunities.

Moving Forward

MINDFULNESS AND STRESS management are essential components of recovery from gambling addiction. Techniques for reducing stress and anxiety, practicing mindfulness and meditation, and maintaining a balanced lifestyle can enhance overall well-being and support long-term success.

Techniques for reducing stress and anxiety include deep breathing exercises, progressive muscle relaxation, visualization and guided imagery, physical exercise, journaling and expressive writing, social support and connection, and time management and organization. These strategies can help create a more serene and controlled life.

Practicing mindfulness and meditation involves understanding mindfulness, basic mindfulness meditation, body scan meditation, loving-kindness meditation, guided meditation, mindful movement, and incorporating mindfulness into daily life. These practices promote a sense of presence and reduce stress.

Maintaining a balanced lifestyle involves prioritizing physical health, mental well-being, social connections, and personal growth. A balanced lifestyle enhances resilience, reduces the risk of relapse, and supports long-term recovery.

Integrating mindfulness and stress management into recovery involves developing a routine, setting boundaries, seeking continued support, and monitoring progress. These strategies provide structure, stability, and ongoing motivation for long-term success.

As we continue to explore the various aspects of gambling addiction in this book, we will provide practical strategies and insights to support individuals on their path to recovery. Understanding the importance of mindfulness and stress management is a crucial step in this process, as it equips individuals with the knowledge and tools needed to overcome addiction and rebuild their lives.

Together, we can build a brighter future free from the destructive impact of compulsive gambling. Whether you are personally struggling with gambling addiction or supporting someone who is, know that help is available and recovery is possible. Let us take the next step forward on this journey towards healing and recovery.

Chapter 10: Overcoming Triggers and Urges

Recovery from gambling addiction involves not only stopping the behavior but also managing the triggers and urges that can lead to relapse. Identifying and avoiding triggers, developing effective strategies for coping with cravings, and staying committed to recovery are essential steps in maintaining long-term sobriety. This chapter will explore these areas in depth, providing practical guidance and support for those on the path to recovery.

Identifying and Avoiding Triggers

TRIGGERS ARE EXTERNAL or internal stimuli that provoke the urge to gamble. Identifying and understanding these triggers is the first step in managing them effectively.

1. Recognizing External Triggers:

External triggers are environmental cues that can prompt gambling urges. These triggers can include specific places, people, situations, or even certain times of day.

- Places: Casinos, betting shops, and other gambling venues are obvious external triggers. Additionally, places like bars or social clubs where gambling is common can also trigger the urge to gamble.

- People: Friends or acquaintances who gamble, as well as individuals who may have lent money or supported gambling habits in the past, can be significant triggers. Social pressure or encouragement to gamble can be challenging to resist.

- Situations: Certain situations, such as social events, sporting events, or times of boredom, can serve as triggers. The association between these situations and past gambling experiences can be strong.

- Media and Advertising: Exposure to advertisements for gambling, such as online betting ads, casino promotions, or even movies and TV shows that depict gambling, can trigger urges.

2. Recognizing Internal Triggers:

Internal triggers are emotional or psychological states that can lead to gambling urges. These triggers are often linked to underlying emotional issues or stress.

- Emotions: Negative emotions such as stress, anxiety, depression, loneliness, and boredom are common internal triggers. Gambling may have been used as a coping mechanism to escape or numb these feelings.

- Thoughts: Certain thoughts or beliefs can trigger gambling urges. This can include rationalizations like "I deserve a win" or "I can control my gambling this time."

- Physical States: Physical states such as fatigue, hunger, or intoxication can lower inhibitions and increase vulnerability to triggers.

3. Creating a Trigger Inventory:

Creating a trigger inventory involves identifying and listing all known external and internal triggers. This inventory serves as a valuable tool for understanding what prompts gambling urges and developing strategies to manage them.

- Listing Triggers: Write down all the places, people, situations, emotions, thoughts, and physical states that have led to gambling urges in the past. Be as specific as possible.

- Analyzing Patterns: Look for patterns in the trigger inventory. Identifying common themes or recurring situations can help in developing targeted strategies to avoid or manage these triggers.

4. Avoiding External Triggers:

Avoiding external triggers involves making conscious decisions to stay away from environments, people, and situations that can prompt gambling urges.

- Avoiding Gambling Venues: Stay away from casinos, betting shops, and other gambling venues. If possible, take alternative routes to avoid passing by these places.

- Limiting Media Exposure: Reduce exposure to gambling advertisements and media that depict gambling. Use ad blockers online, avoid TV channels with frequent gambling ads, and unfollow social media accounts that promote gambling.

- Setting Boundaries with People: Set clear boundaries with friends or acquaintances who gamble. Explain your situation and request their support in avoiding gambling-related activities. If necessary, distance yourself from individuals who do not respect your boundaries.

- Changing Social Activities: Replace social activities that involve gambling with alternative activities. Find new ways to socialize and have fun without the risk of encountering gambling triggers.

5. Managing Internal Triggers:

Managing internal triggers involves developing healthy coping mechanisms to deal with emotions, thoughts, and physical states that can lead to gambling urges.

- Emotional Regulation: Practice emotional regulation techniques such as mindfulness, deep breathing, journaling, or talking to a therapist. Developing healthy ways to process and cope with emotions reduces the reliance on gambling as an escape.

- Cognitive Restructuring: Challenge and reframe thoughts that lead to gambling urges. Replace irrational beliefs with more realistic and positive thoughts. For example, instead of thinking "I need to gamble to feel better," reframe it to "I can find healthier ways to cope with my emotions."

- Physical Self-Care: Take care of your physical well-being by getting enough sleep, eating nutritious meals, and avoiding excessive alcohol or drug use. Physical self-care supports overall resilience and reduces vulnerability to triggers.

6. Creating a Trigger Management Plan:

A trigger management plan is a proactive approach to handling triggers and avoiding relapse. This plan includes specific strategies for avoiding and managing identified triggers.

- Avoidance Strategies: Outline specific actions you will take to avoid external triggers. This can include changing your routine, avoiding certain places, and setting boundaries with people.

- Coping Strategies: Identify healthy coping mechanisms for managing internal triggers. This can include practicing mindfulness, engaging in physical exercise, or seeking support from a therapist or support group.

- Emergency Plan: Develop an emergency plan for handling unexpected triggers or intense urges. This plan can include contacting a trusted friend or support group member, practicing deep breathing exercises, or removing yourself from the triggering situation.

Strategies for Coping with Cravings

CRAVINGS ARE INTENSE urges to gamble that can be difficult to resist. Developing effective strategies for coping with cravings is essential for maintaining sobriety and preventing relapse.

1. Understanding Cravings:

Cravings are a natural part of the recovery process and do not indicate failure. Understanding the nature of cravings can help in managing them effectively.

- Temporary Nature: Recognize that cravings are temporary and will pass. They typically peak and then subside, often within 20-30 minutes. Remind yourself that you can ride out the craving without giving in.

- Physiological Basis: Cravings have a physiological basis and are often triggered by changes in brain chemistry. Understanding this can help you depersonalize the experience and view it as a normal part of recovery.

2. Distracting Yourself:

Distraction is an effective way to cope with cravings. Engaging in alternative activities can shift your focus and reduce the intensity of the urge.

- Engage in Hobbies: Dive into hobbies or activities that you enjoy, such as reading, painting, playing a musical instrument, or gardening. These activities can provide a positive and fulfilling alternative to gambling.

- Exercise: Physical exercise is a great way to distract yourself from cravings. Go for a run, take a walk, practice yoga, or engage in any physical activity that gets your body moving and releases endorphins.

- Social Interaction: Spend time with friends or family members who support your recovery. Engaging in positive social interactions can provide emotional support and reduce the intensity of cravings.

3. Practicing Mindfulness:

Mindfulness involves paying attention to the present moment without judgment. Practicing mindfulness can help you observe and manage cravings without acting on them.

- Mindful Breathing: Focus on your breath and observe the sensations of each inhale and exhale. If your mind wanders, gently bring your attention back to your breath. This practice can help you stay grounded and reduce the intensity of cravings.

- Body Scan: Perform a body scan by bringing your attention to different parts of your body, starting from your toes and moving up to your head. Notice any areas of tension or discomfort and allow them to relax. This practice can help you connect with your body and reduce the urge to gamble.

- Observing Thoughts: Notice the thoughts that arise during a craving without judgment. Observe them as passing events rather than facts. This practice can help you distance yourself from the urge and reduce its power.

4. Using Cognitive Techniques:

Cognitive techniques involve challenging and reframing the thoughts that lead to cravings. These techniques can help you develop a more rational and balanced perspective.

- Cognitive Restructuring: Identify and challenge irrational thoughts that lead to cravings. Replace them with more realistic and positive thoughts. For example, if you think "I can't handle this craving," reframe it to "I have successfully managed cravings before and can do it again."

- Thought Stopping: When you notice a craving-related thought, use a thought-stopping technique to interrupt it. This can include saying "Stop!" out loud or visualizing a stop sign. Then, replace the thought with a more positive and constructive one.

- Reality Testing: Test the reality of craving-related thoughts by examining the evidence for and against them. For example, if you think "I need to gamble to feel better," consider the negative consequences of gambling and the positive alternatives available.

5. Building a Support Network:

Having a strong support network can provide encouragement, accountability, and emotional support during cravings.

- Support Groups: Participate in support groups such as Gamblers Anonymous or SMART Recovery. These groups provide a sense of community and shared understanding, which can be invaluable during challenging times.

- Therapy: Work with a therapist who specializes in addiction recovery. A therapist can provide personalized strategies and support for managing cravings and maintaining sobriety.

- Trusted Friends and Family: Reach out to trusted friends or family members who support your recovery. Let them know when you are experiencing cravings and ask for their support and encouragement.

6. Developing Coping Skills:

Developing healthy coping skills can help you manage stress and emotions without resorting to gambling.

- Stress Management: Practice stress management techniques such as deep breathing, meditation, progressive muscle relaxation, or visualization. These techniques can help you stay calm and centered during stressful situations.

- Emotional Regulation: Develop healthy ways to process and cope with emotions. This can include journaling, talking to a therapist, or engaging in creative outlets.

- Problem-Solving: Develop problem-solving skills to address the challenges and stressors in your life. Break down problems into manageable steps and develop actionable solutions.

7. Using Relapse Prevention Strategies:

Relapse prevention strategies involve planning for and managing situations that could lead to relapse. These strategies can help you stay committed to your recovery and reduce the risk of giving in to cravings.

- Identifying High-Risk Situations: Identify situations that are likely to trigger cravings and develop a plan for managing them. This can include social events, stressful situations, or specific times of day.

- Developing a Relapse Prevention Plan: Create a relapse prevention plan that outlines specific actions you will take to avoid and manage high-risk situations. This plan can include strategies for avoiding triggers, coping with cravings, and seeking support.

- Practicing Self-Care: Prioritize self-care to maintain physical, mental, and emotional well-being. Taking care of yourself reduces vulnerability to cravings and supports long-term recovery.

Staying Committed to Recovery

STAYING COMMITTED TO recovery involves maintaining motivation, setting goals, and developing a mindset that supports long-term sobriety. It requires ongoing effort and dedication to overcome challenges and stay on the path to recovery.

1. Maintaining Motivation:

Maintaining motivation is essential for staying committed to recovery. Finding and nurturing sources of motivation can help you stay focused and determined.

- Identifying Reasons for Recovery: Identify and write down the reasons why you want to recover from gambling addiction. These reasons can include improving your health, repairing relationships, achieving financial stability, and finding personal fulfillment. Keep this list visible and refer to it when you need a reminder of why you are committed to recovery.

- Visualizing Success: Visualize yourself successfully overcoming gambling addiction and achieving your goals. Create a mental image of the positive changes in your life as a result of your recovery. This visualization can provide inspiration and motivation.

- Celebrating Milestones: Celebrate milestones and achievements along your recovery journey. Recognize and reward yourself for your hard work and progress. Celebrating successes can reinforce positive behavior and boost motivation.

2. Setting and Achieving Goals:

Setting and achieving goals can provide structure and direction in your recovery journey. Goals give you something to work towards and can help you stay focused and motivated.

- Setting SMART Goals: Set goals that are Specific, Measurable, Achievable, Relevant, and Time-bound (SMART). These criteria ensure that your goals are clear, realistic, and actionable.

- Breaking Down Goals: Break larger goals into smaller, manageable steps. This makes the goals less overwhelming and allows you to track your progress more easily.

- Reviewing and Adjusting Goals: Regularly review your goals and adjust them based on your progress and changing circumstances. Be flexible and willing to adapt your goals as needed.

3. Developing a Positive Mindset:

Developing a positive mindset can help you stay committed to recovery and overcome challenges. A positive mindset involves focusing on strengths, practicing gratitude, and maintaining a hopeful outlook.

- Focusing on Strengths: Identify and focus on your strengths and positive qualities. Recognize the skills and abilities that have helped you in your recovery journey.

- Practicing Gratitude: Practice gratitude by regularly reflecting on the positive aspects of your life. Keep a gratitude journal and write down things you are grateful for each day. This practice can shift your focus from challenges to positive experiences.

- Maintaining Hope: Maintain a hopeful outlook and believe in your ability to overcome challenges. Remind yourself that recovery is a journey and that setbacks are a natural part of the process.

4. Building Resilience:

Building resilience involves developing the ability to bounce back from setbacks and challenges. Resilience is essential for staying committed to recovery and maintaining long-term sobriety.

- Developing Coping Skills: Develop healthy coping skills for managing stress, emotions, and challenges. This can include mindfulness, deep breathing, journaling, and seeking support from others.

- Practicing Self-Compassion: Practice self-compassion by treating yourself with kindness and understanding. Recognize that setbacks are a normal part of recovery and do not define your worth or ability to succeed.

- Learning from Setbacks: View setbacks as opportunities for learning and growth. Reflect on what you can learn from the experience and how you can use this knowledge to strengthen your recovery.

5. Seeking Support:

Seeking support from others is essential for staying committed to recovery. Support provides encouragement, accountability, and emotional strength.

- Support Groups: Continue participating in support groups, such as Gamblers Anonymous or SMART Recovery. These groups provide a sense of community and shared understanding.

- Therapy: Maintain regular therapy sessions to address ongoing challenges and develop new coping strategies. Therapy provides personalized support and guidance.

- Loved Ones: Stay connected with loved ones who support your recovery. Communicate openly and seek their encouragement and understanding.

6. Practicing Self-Care:

Practicing self-care is essential for maintaining physical, mental, and emotional well-being. Self-care reduces vulnerability to cravings and supports long-term recovery.

- Physical Self-Care: Prioritize regular exercise, proper nutrition, and adequate sleep. Physical self-care enhances overall well-being and resilience.

- Emotional Self-Care: Develop healthy ways to process and cope with emotions. This can include journaling, talking to a therapist, or engaging in creative outlets.

- Mental Self-Care: Engage in activities that stimulate and challenge your mind. This can include reading, learning new skills, or participating in hobbies and interests.

Moving Forward

OVERCOMING TRIGGERS and urges is a critical component of recovery from gambling addiction. Identifying and avoiding triggers, developing effective strategies for coping with cravings, and staying committed to recovery are essential steps in maintaining long-term sobriety.

Identifying and avoiding triggers involves recognizing external and internal triggers, creating a trigger inventory, avoiding external triggers, and managing internal triggers. Developing a trigger management plan provides a proactive approach to handling triggers and reducing the risk of relapse.

Strategies for coping with cravings include understanding cravings, distracting yourself, practicing mindfulness, using cognitive techniques, building a support network, developing coping skills, and using relapse prevention strategies. These techniques help manage cravings effectively and support long-term recovery.

Staying committed to recovery involves maintaining motivation, setting and achieving goals, developing a positive mindset, building resilience, seeking support, and practicing self-care. These strategies provide structure, direction, and ongoing motivation for long-term success.

As we continue to explore the various aspects of gambling addiction in this book, we will provide practical strategies and insights to support individuals on their path to recovery. Understanding the importance of overcoming triggers and urges is a crucial step in this process, as it equips individuals with the knowledge and tools needed to overcome addiction and rebuild their lives.

Together, we can build a brighter future free from the destructive impact of compulsive gambling. Whether you are personally struggling with gambling addiction or supporting someone who is, know that help is available and recovery is possible. Let us take the next step forward on this journey towards healing and recovery.

Chapter 11: Therapy and Counseling Options

———

Therapy and counseling are fundamental components of recovery from gambling addiction. They offer structured support, professional guidance, and effective strategies to address the underlying causes of addiction and develop healthier coping mechanisms. This chapter explores cognitive-behavioral therapy (CBT), group therapy and peer support, and other therapeutic approaches that can be beneficial in overcoming gambling addiction.

Cognitive-Behavioral Therapy (CBT)

COGNITIVE-BEHAVIORAL therapy (CBT) is one of the most widely used and effective therapeutic approaches for treating gambling addiction. It focuses on identifying and changing the negative thought patterns and behaviors that contribute to the addiction.

1. Understanding CBT:

CBT is a structured, time-limited therapy that typically involves 12-20 sessions. It is based on the idea that our thoughts, feelings, and behaviors are interconnected and that changing negative thought patterns can lead to changes in behavior and emotional state.

- Principles of CBT: CBT is grounded in the principles of cognitive restructuring and behavioral activation. Cognitive restructuring involves identifying and challenging irrational or unhelpful thoughts, while behavioral activation focuses on changing behaviors to improve mood and functioning.

- Goals of CBT: The primary goals of CBT in treating gambling addiction are to reduce gambling behaviors, address the underlying cognitive distortions, and develop healthier coping mechanisms. CBT also aims to improve overall mental health and quality of life.

2. Cognitive Restructuring:

Cognitive restructuring is a core component of CBT that involves identifying and challenging irrational or unhelpful thoughts related to gambling.

- Identifying Cognitive Distortions: Cognitive distortions are irrational or biased ways of thinking that can contribute to gambling addiction. Common distortions in gambling include the illusion of control (believing one can control random outcomes), the gambler's fallacy (believing that past losses influence future wins), and selective memory (remembering wins more than losses).

- Challenging Irrational Thoughts: Once cognitive distortions are identified, the next step is to challenge and reframe these thoughts. This involves examining the evidence for and against the thought, considering alternative perspectives, and developing more balanced and realistic thoughts. For example, replacing the thought "I can win back my losses if I keep playing" with "Gambling is a game of chance, and continuing to play will likely lead to more losses."

- Developing Positive Thinking Patterns: Cognitive restructuring aims to replace negative thought patterns with more positive and constructive thinking. This can help reduce the urge to gamble and improve overall mental well-being.

3. Behavioral Activation:

Behavioral activation focuses on changing behaviors to improve mood and functioning. It involves identifying and engaging in positive activities that can replace gambling.

- Activity Scheduling: Activity scheduling involves planning and engaging in positive activities that provide enjoyment and fulfillment. This can include hobbies, social activities, exercise, and relaxation techniques. Scheduling activities helps to fill the time previously spent on gambling and provides alternative sources of pleasure.

- Behavioral Experiments: Behavioral experiments are structured activities designed to test the validity of negative thoughts and beliefs. For example, if a person believes that they cannot have fun without gambling, they might plan an enjoyable activity without gambling and observe their experience. This can help challenge and change negative beliefs.

- Increasing Positive Reinforcement: Behavioral activation aims to increase positive reinforcement by engaging in activities that provide a sense of accomplishment and satisfaction. This can help improve mood and reduce the reliance on gambling for pleasure.

4. Coping Skills Training:

CBT includes training in coping skills to manage stress, emotions, and triggers that can lead to gambling.

- Stress Management: Stress management techniques, such as deep breathing, progressive muscle relaxation, and mindfulness, can help reduce the physiological and psychological effects of stress. These techniques can be used to manage cravings and reduce the urge to gamble.

- Emotional Regulation: Emotional regulation skills involve identifying and managing emotions in healthy ways. This can include journaling, talking to a therapist, or engaging in creative outlets. Developing emotional regulation skills can reduce the reliance on gambling as a coping mechanism.

- Problem-Solving Skills: Problem-solving skills involve identifying and addressing challenges and stressors in a constructive way. This can include breaking down problems into manageable steps, generating and evaluating solutions, and implementing action plans. Effective problem-solving can reduce the stress and frustration that can lead to gambling.

5. Relapse Prevention:

Relapse prevention is an essential component of CBT that involves identifying high-risk situations and developing strategies to manage them.

- Identifying Triggers: Identifying triggers involves recognizing the situations, people, and emotions that can lead to gambling urges. This can include external triggers, such as visiting a casino, and internal triggers, such as feelings of boredom or stress.

- Developing Coping Strategies: Developing coping strategies involves creating a plan for managing triggers and cravings. This can include avoiding high-risk situations, using stress management techniques, and seeking support from others.

- Building Resilience: Building resilience involves developing the skills and resources needed to cope with challenges and setbacks. This can include practicing self-care, seeking social support, and maintaining a positive mindset. Building resilience can help reduce the risk of relapse and support long-term recovery.

Group Therapy and Peer Support

GROUP THERAPY AND PEER support provide a sense of community and shared understanding, which can be invaluable in the recovery process. These approaches offer emotional support, accountability, and practical advice from others who have experienced similar challenges.

1. Understanding Group Therapy:

Group therapy involves regular meetings with a therapist and a group of individuals who are also recovering from gambling addiction. It provides a supportive environment for sharing experiences, discussing challenges, and developing coping strategies.

- Benefits of Group Therapy: Group therapy offers several benefits, including social support, reduced feelings of isolation, opportunities for learning from others, and a sense of accountability. Sharing experiences with others who understand the challenges of addiction can provide validation and encouragement.

- Structure of Group Therapy: Group therapy sessions typically involve a combination of discussion, skill-building activities, and support. The therapist facilitates the group, encourages participation, and ensures a safe and respectful environment.

2. Types of Group Therapy:

There are several types of group therapy that can be beneficial for individuals recovering from gambling addiction.

- Psychoeducational Groups: Psychoeducational groups provide information about gambling addiction, its effects, and strategies for recovery. These groups focus on education and skill-building, helping participants develop a better understanding of their addiction and learn practical coping strategies.

- Support Groups: Support groups provide a space for participants to share their experiences, challenges, and successes in a supportive environment. These groups emphasize mutual support and encouragement, helping participants feel less alone in their recovery journey.

- Cognitive-Behavioral Groups: Cognitive-behavioral groups focus on the principles of CBT, helping participants identify and change negative thought patterns and behaviors. These groups provide structured activities and exercises to support cognitive restructuring and behavioral activation.

- Relapse Prevention Groups: Relapse prevention groups focus on identifying high-risk situations and developing strategies to manage them. These groups provide tools and techniques for maintaining sobriety and preventing relapse.

3. Peer Support Programs:

Peer support programs involve individuals who are in recovery from gambling addiction providing support and guidance to others who are also recovering. These programs emphasize the value of lived experience and mutual support.

- Gamblers Anonymous (GA): Gamblers Anonymous is a 12-step program modeled after Alcoholics Anonymous. It involves regular meetings where participants share their experiences, work through the 12 steps, and provide support to one another. GA emphasizes the importance of accountability, self-awareness, and spiritual growth in recovery.

- SMART Recovery: SMART Recovery (Self-Management and Recovery Training) is an alternative to the 12-step approach. It focuses on self-empowerment and self-reliance, using evidence-based techniques from CBT and motivational interviewing. SMART Recovery meetings provide a structured environment for discussing challenges, setting goals, and developing coping strategies.

- Online Support Groups: Online support groups and forums provide a convenient and accessible way to connect with others who are recovering from gambling addiction. These platforms offer anonymity and flexibility, making it easier for individuals to seek support regardless of their location or schedule.

4. Building a Support Network:

Building a support network involves creating a circle of individuals who provide encouragement, accountability, and emotional support. This network can include friends, family members, therapists, and peers in recovery.

- Choosing Supportive Individuals: Choose individuals who are understanding, non-judgmental, and supportive of your recovery. This can include friends and family members who respect your boundaries and encourage positive behavior.

- Maintaining Communication: Regular communication with your support network is essential for maintaining motivation and addressing challenges. Share your progress, discuss challenges, and seek advice and encouragement.

- Participating in Group Activities: Engaging in group activities and social events with your support network can provide positive reinforcement and reduce feelings of isolation. These activities can include attending support group meetings, participating in recreational activities, and celebrating milestones.

Exploring Other Therapeutic Approaches

IN ADDITION TO CBT and group therapy, there are several other therapeutic approaches that can be beneficial in treating gambling addiction. These approaches offer diverse perspectives and techniques for addressing the underlying causes of addiction and supporting long-term recovery.

1. Motivational Interviewing (MI):

Motivational interviewing is a therapeutic approach that helps individuals resolve ambivalence about change and enhance their motivation for recovery. It is based on the principles of collaboration, evocation, and autonomy.

- Principles of MI: MI emphasizes the importance of empathy, non-judgment, and active listening. The therapist works collaboratively with the individual to explore their motivations for change and develop a personalized plan for recovery.

- Techniques of MI: MI techniques include open-ended questions, reflective listening, affirmations, and summarizing. These techniques help individuals articulate their goals, identify barriers to change, and develop a sense of self-efficacy.

- Applications of MI:

MI is particularly effective in the early stages of recovery, helping individuals build motivation and commitment to change. It can also be used in conjunction with other therapeutic approaches, such as CBT, to support long-term recovery.

2. Dialectical Behavior Therapy (DBT):

Dialectical behavior therapy is a form of CBT that focuses on emotional regulation, distress tolerance, interpersonal effectiveness, and mindfulness. DBT was originally developed to treat borderline personality disorder but has been adapted for use with various addictive behaviors, including gambling.

- Components of DBT: DBT consists of individual therapy, group skills training, phone coaching, and therapist consultation. These components provide comprehensive support and skill-building for individuals in recovery.

- Skills Training in DBT: DBT skills training focuses on four key areas: mindfulness, distress tolerance, emotional regulation, and interpersonal effectiveness. These skills help individuals manage emotions, cope with stress, and build healthy relationships.

- Applications of DBT: DBT is particularly effective for individuals who struggle with intense emotions, impulsivity, and self-destructive behaviors. It provides practical tools for managing cravings, reducing the urge to gamble, and building a balanced and fulfilling life.

3. Acceptance and Commitment Therapy (ACT):

Acceptance and commitment therapy is a therapeutic approach that combines mindfulness and behavioral change strategies. ACT focuses on helping individuals accept their thoughts and feelings, commit to values-based actions, and develop psychological flexibility.

- Principles of ACT: ACT is based on six core processes: acceptance, cognitive defusion, being present, self-as-context, values, and committed action. These processes help individuals develop a more flexible and adaptive approach to their thoughts and behaviors.

- Techniques of ACT: ACT techniques include mindfulness exercises, values clarification, and commitment strategies. These techniques help individuals accept their experiences, distance themselves from unhelpful thoughts, and take actions that align with their values.

- Applications of ACT: ACT is effective for individuals who struggle with avoidance and rigid thinking. It provides tools for managing cravings, reducing the impact of negative thoughts, and building a meaningful and values-driven life.

4. Psychodynamic Therapy:

Psychodynamic therapy focuses on exploring the unconscious processes and unresolved conflicts that contribute to addictive behaviors. It aims to increase self-awareness and insight, helping individuals understand the underlying causes of their addiction.

- Principles of Psychodynamic Therapy: Psychodynamic therapy emphasizes the importance of early experiences, unconscious motivations, and relational dynamics. The therapist works with the individual to explore and understand these factors.

- Techniques of Psychodynamic Therapy: Techniques include free association, dream analysis, and exploration of transference and countertransference. These techniques help individuals gain insight into their unconscious processes and develop healthier patterns of behavior.

- Applications of Psychodynamic Therapy: Psychodynamic therapy is particularly effective for individuals who have deep-seated emotional issues and unresolved conflicts. It provides a comprehensive approach to understanding and addressing the root causes of addiction.

5. Integrative and Holistic Approaches:

Integrative and holistic approaches combine multiple therapeutic modalities to address the physical, mental, emotional, and spiritual aspects of addiction. These approaches recognize the interconnectedness of mind, body, and spirit and aim to promote overall well-being.

- Integrative Therapy: Integrative therapy involves combining different therapeutic techniques and approaches to create a personalized treatment plan. This can include elements of CBT, MI, ACT, DBT, and other therapies.

- Holistic Approaches: Holistic approaches may include complementary and alternative therapies, such as acupuncture, yoga, meditation, nutrition counseling, and spiritual practices. These therapies aim to support overall health and well-being and provide additional tools for managing cravings and stress.

- Applications of Integrative and Holistic Approaches: Integrative and holistic approaches are effective for individuals who seek a comprehensive and individualized treatment plan. They provide diverse tools and techniques for addressing the multifaceted nature of addiction and supporting long-term recovery.

Moving Forward

THERAPY AND COUNSELING are essential components of recovery from gambling addiction. Cognitive-behavioral therapy (CBT), group therapy and peer support, and other therapeutic approaches offer structured support, professional guidance, and effective strategies for overcoming addiction and building a fulfilling life.

CBT focuses on identifying and changing negative thought patterns and behaviors, developing healthier coping mechanisms, and preventing relapse. Group therapy and peer support provide a sense of community and shared understanding, offering emotional support, accountability, and practical advice. Other therapeutic approaches, such as motivational interviewing, dialectical behavior therapy, acceptance and commitment therapy, psychodynamic therapy, and integrative and holistic approaches, offer diverse perspectives and techniques for addressing the underlying causes of addiction and supporting long-term recovery.

As we continue to explore the various aspects of gambling addiction in this book, we will provide practical strategies and insights to support individuals on their path to recovery. Understanding the importance of therapy and counseling options is a crucial step in this process, as it equips individuals with the knowledge and tools needed to overcome addiction and rebuild their lives.

Together, we can build a brighter future free from the destructive impact of compulsive gambling. Whether you are personally struggling with gambling addiction or supporting someone who is, know that help is available and recovery is possible. Let us take the next step forward on this journey towards healing and recovery.

Chapter 12: Relapse Prevention

———

Relapse is a common and often expected part of the recovery process from gambling addiction. Understanding relapse as part of recovery, developing strategies for maintaining progress, and knowing what to do if a relapse occurs are crucial for long-term success. This chapter explores these aspects in depth, providing comprehensive guidance and practical strategies to support individuals on their journey to recovery.

Understanding Relapse as Part of Recovery

RELAPSE IS A RETURN to gambling behavior after a period of abstinence. It is important to recognize that relapse does not signify failure but is a part of the recovery process for many individuals. Understanding the nature of relapse can help in developing effective prevention strategies and fostering a resilient mindset.

1. The Nature of Relapse:

Relapse is a process rather than a single event. It often begins with emotional and mental changes that precede the physical act of gambling.

- Emotional Relapse: During emotional relapse, individuals may experience negative emotions such as stress, anxiety, or frustration. They might not be consciously thinking about gambling but are setting the stage for a potential relapse by neglecting self-care and healthy coping mechanisms.

- Mental Relapse: Mental relapse involves an internal struggle where part of the individual wants to gamble, while the other part resists. Thoughts about gambling, romanticizing past gambling experiences, and seeking opportunities to gamble characterize this stage.

- Physical Relapse: Physical relapse is the actual return to gambling behavior. It is the culmination of the emotional and mental relapse processes.

2. Factors Contributing to Relapse:

Several factors can contribute to the risk of relapse. Understanding these factors can help in developing strategies to manage them effectively.

- Stress: High levels of stress can trigger a relapse. Stressful situations, whether related to work, relationships, or finances, can increase the urge to gamble as a coping mechanism.

- Negative Emotions: Feelings of sadness, anger, loneliness, or boredom can contribute to relapse. Gambling may have previously been used to escape or numb these emotions.

- Environmental Cues: Exposure to places, people, or situations associated with past gambling behavior can trigger relapse. These environmental cues can evoke strong urges to gamble.

- Lack of Support: Insufficient support from family, friends, or support groups can increase the risk of relapse. A strong support network is crucial for maintaining motivation and accountability.

- Complacency: Over time, individuals may become complacent about their recovery, believing they are no longer at risk of relapse. This complacency can lead to neglecting self-care and relapse prevention strategies.

3. Viewing Relapse as a Learning Opportunity:

It is essential to view relapse as a learning opportunity rather than a failure. Analyzing the factors that led to the relapse and developing strategies to address them can strengthen the recovery process.

- Identifying Triggers: Reflect on the specific triggers that contributed to the relapse. Understanding these triggers can help in developing targeted strategies to manage them in the future.

- Evaluating Coping Mechanisms: Assess the effectiveness of the coping mechanisms used during the relapse. Identify which strategies were helpful and which were not, and consider incorporating new techniques.

- Adjusting the Recovery Plan: Use the insights gained from the relapse to adjust the recovery plan. This may involve enhancing support systems, incorporating additional coping strategies, or seeking professional help.

Strategies for Maintaining Progress

MAINTAINING PROGRESS in recovery requires ongoing effort, commitment, and the implementation of effective strategies. These strategies help to strengthen resilience, manage triggers and cravings, and support long-term sobriety.

1. Building a Strong Support Network:

A strong support network provides encouragement, accountability, and emotional support. Engaging with supportive individuals and groups can enhance motivation and reduce the risk of relapse.

- Family and Friends: Communicate openly with trusted family members and friends about your recovery journey. Their understanding and support can be invaluable in maintaining progress.

- Support Groups: Participate in support groups such as Gamblers Anonymous or SMART Recovery. These groups offer a sense of community and shared understanding, which can be vital for ongoing support.

- Therapists and Counselors: Work with a therapist or counselor who specializes in addiction recovery. Professional guidance can help address underlying issues and develop effective coping strategies.

2. Developing Healthy Coping Mechanisms:

Healthy coping mechanisms are essential for managing stress, emotions, and triggers without resorting to gambling.

- Stress Management: Practice stress management techniques such as deep breathing, progressive muscle relaxation, mindfulness, and physical exercise. These techniques can help reduce the physiological and psychological effects of stress.

- Emotional Regulation: Develop healthy ways to process and cope with emotions. This can include journaling, talking to a therapist, or engaging in creative outlets.

- Problem-Solving Skills: Develop problem-solving skills to address challenges and stressors constructively. This can include breaking down problems into manageable steps, generating and evaluating solutions, and implementing action plans.

3. Setting and Achieving Goals:

Setting and achieving goals provides structure, direction, and a sense of accomplishment in the recovery journey.

- SMART Goals: Set goals that are Specific, Measurable, Achievable, Relevant, and Time-bound (SMART). These criteria ensure that your goals are clear, realistic, and actionable.

- Short-Term and Long-Term Goals: Set both short-term and long-term goals to guide your recovery. Short-term goals focus on immediate needs and provide quick wins, while long-term goals focus on broader aspirations and sustained progress.

- Regular Review and Adjustment: Regularly review and adjust your goals based on your progress and changing circumstances. Be flexible and willing to adapt your goals as needed.

4. Practicing Mindfulness and Self-Care:

Mindfulness and self-care practices promote overall well-being and reduce vulnerability to relapse.

- Mindfulness: Practice mindfulness techniques such as mindful breathing, body scan, and mindful movement. These practices help you stay present, manage stress, and reduce the intensity of cravings.

- Self-Care: Prioritize self-care by engaging in activities that promote physical, mental, and emotional well-being. This can include regular exercise, a balanced diet, adequate sleep, and relaxation activities.

- Balanced Lifestyle: Maintain a balanced lifestyle by integrating work, self-care, social activities, and personal growth. A balanced lifestyle supports overall health and resilience.

5. Avoiding High-Risk Situations:

Avoiding high-risk situations involves making conscious decisions to stay away from environments, people, and situations that can trigger gambling urges.

- Identifying High-Risk Situations: Identify situations that are likely to trigger cravings and develop a plan for managing them. This can include social events, stressful situations, or specific times of day.

- Setting Boundaries: Set clear boundaries with friends or acquaintances who gamble. Explain your situation and request their support in avoiding gambling-related activities.

- Changing Routines: Adjust your daily routines to reduce exposure to triggers. This can include taking alternative routes to avoid passing by gambling venues and finding new ways to socialize and have fun.

6. Developing a Relapse Prevention Plan:

A relapse prevention plan is a proactive approach to managing triggers and reducing the risk of relapse.

- Trigger Management: Outline specific actions you will take to avoid and manage identified triggers. This can include avoiding high-risk situations, using stress management techniques, and seeking support from others.

- Coping Strategies: Identify healthy coping mechanisms for managing cravings and stress. This can include practicing mindfulness, engaging in physical exercise, or seeking support from a therapist or support group.

- Emergency Plan: Develop an emergency plan for handling unexpected triggers or intense urges. This plan can include contacting a trusted friend or support group member, practicing deep breathing exercises, or removing yourself from the triggering situation.

What to Do If a Relapse Occurs

Relapse is a common part of the recovery process, and knowing how to respond if it occurs is crucial for getting back on track. Taking immediate action, seeking support, and learning from the experience can help strengthen your recovery.

1. Taking Immediate Action:

If a relapse occurs, taking immediate action can help minimize its impact and prevent further gambling behavior.

- Stop Gambling Immediately: Cease all gambling activities as soon as you recognize that you have relapsed. The longer you continue, the more difficult it will be to stop.

- Remove Access to Gambling: Remove access to gambling opportunities by blocking online gambling sites, deleting gambling apps, and avoiding gambling venues. Limiting access can reduce the temptation to continue gambling.

- Seek Immediate Support: Contact a trusted friend, family member, or support group member for immediate support and encouragement. Talking to someone who understands your situation can provide emotional relief and help you refocus on your recovery.

2. Reflecting on the Relapse:

Reflecting on the relapse involves analyzing the factors that led to it and identifying lessons that can be applied to strengthen your recovery.

- Identifying Triggers: Reflect on the specific triggers that contributed to the relapse. Understanding these triggers can help in developing targeted strategies to manage them in the future.

- Evaluating Coping Mechanisms: Assess the effectiveness of the coping mechanisms used during the relapse. Identify which strategies were helpful and which were not, and consider incorporating new techniques.

- Analyzing the Relapse Process: Consider the emotional, mental, and behavioral stages that led to the relapse. Understanding this process can provide insights into how to intervene earlier and prevent future relapses.

3. Seeking Professional Help:

Seeking professional help can provide valuable guidance and support in recovering from a relapse and strengthening your recovery plan.

- Therapist or Counselor: Work with a therapist or counselor who specializes in addiction recovery. They can help you address underlying issues, develop effective coping strategies, and rebuild your confidence in your ability to maintain sobriety.

- Support Groups: Continue participating in support groups such as Gamblers Anonymous or SMART Recovery. These groups provide a sense of community and shared understanding, which can be vital for ongoing support.

- Relapse Prevention Programs: Consider enrolling in a relapse prevention program or workshop that provides structured guidance and support for managing triggers and maintaining sobriety.

4. Adjusting the Recovery Plan:

Use the insights gained from the relapse to adjust your recovery plan and strengthen your commitment to sobriety.

- Enhancing Support Systems: Strengthen your support systems by increasing participation in support groups, seeking additional therapy, and building a stronger network of supportive individuals.

- Incorporating New Strategies: Incorporate new coping strategies and techniques to manage triggers and cravings more effectively. This can include mindfulness practices, stress management techniques, and self-care activities.

- Setting New Goals: Set new recovery goals that reflect your renewed commitment to sobriety. These goals can provide motivation and direction in your recovery journey.

5. Building Resilience:

Building resilience involves developing the ability to bounce back from setbacks and challenges. Resilience is essential for staying committed to recovery and maintaining long-term sobriety.

- Developing Coping Skills: Develop healthy coping skills for managing stress, emotions, and challenges. This can include mindfulness, deep breathing, journaling, and seeking support from others.

- Practicing Self-Compassion: Practice self-compassion by treating yourself with kindness and understanding. Recognize that setbacks are a normal part of recovery and do not define your worth or ability to succeed.

- Learning from Setbacks: View setbacks as opportunities for learning and growth. Reflect on what you can learn from the experience and how you can use this knowledge to strengthen your recovery.

Moving Forward

RELAPSE PREVENTION is a critical component of recovery from gambling addiction. Understanding relapse as part of recovery, developing strategies for maintaining progress, and knowing what to do if a relapse occurs are essential steps in maintaining long-term sobriety.

Understanding relapse as part of recovery involves recognizing the nature of relapse, identifying factors that contribute to it, and viewing it as a learning opportunity. This perspective helps to reduce the stigma associated with relapse and fosters a resilient mindset.

Strategies for maintaining progress include building a strong support network, developing healthy coping mechanisms, setting and achieving goals, practicing mindfulness and self-care, avoiding high-risk situations, and developing a relapse prevention plan. These strategies provide structure, direction, and ongoing motivation for long-term success.

Knowing what to do if a relapse occurs involves taking immediate action, reflecting on the relapse, seeking professional help, adjusting the recovery plan, and building resilience. These steps help to minimize the impact of relapse and support continued progress in recovery.

As we continue to explore the various aspects of gambling addiction in this book, we will provide practical strategies and insights to support individuals on their path to recovery. Understanding the importance of relapse prevention is a crucial step in this process, as it equips individuals with the knowledge and tools needed to overcome addiction and rebuild their lives.

Together, we can build a brighter future free from the destructive impact of compulsive gambling. Whether you are personally struggling with gambling addiction or supporting someone who is, know that help is available and recovery is possible. Let us take the next step forward on this journey towards healing and recovery.

Chapter 13: Strengthening Relationships

Gambling addiction often strains relationships, leading to broken trust, poor communication, and emotional distance. Rebuilding these relationships is crucial for both personal recovery and overall well-being. This chapter explores how to rebuild trust with loved ones, effective communication strategies, and the benefits of participating in family therapy.

Rebuilding Trust with Loved Ones

TRUST IS THE FOUNDATION of any healthy relationship, and rebuilding it after the damage caused by gambling addiction requires time, effort, and consistency. Here are the steps and strategies to rebuild trust with loved ones.

1. Acknowledging the Damage:

The first step in rebuilding trust is to acknowledge the damage caused by gambling addiction. This involves being honest about the behaviors and decisions that have hurt your loved ones.

- Taking Responsibility: Accept full responsibility for your actions and the impact they have had on your loved ones. Avoid making excuses or blaming others for your behavior. Acknowledging your mistakes shows that you understand the gravity of the situation.

- Apologizing Sincerely: Offer a sincere apology to your loved ones. Express genuine remorse for the hurt and pain you have caused. A heartfelt apology can be the first step in healing and rebuilding trust.

2. Making Amends:

Making amends involves taking specific actions to address the harm caused by your gambling addiction. This can include financial restitution, rebuilding emotional connections, and restoring stability in the relationship.

- Financial Restitution: If your gambling addiction has led to financial harm, develop a plan to repay any debts or financial losses. This may involve creating a budget, seeking financial counseling, and making regular payments. Demonstrating a commitment to financial responsibility can help rebuild trust.

- Emotional Connection: Rebuilding emotional connections involves spending quality time with your loved ones, engaging in meaningful conversations, and showing empathy and understanding. Prioritize their needs and concerns and work towards rebuilding a sense of closeness and connection.

- Restoring Stability: Work on restoring stability in your relationships by being consistent, reliable, and dependable. Follow through on commitments and promises, and demonstrate that you are working towards positive change.

3. Demonstrating Consistency and Transparency:

Consistency and transparency are key to rebuilding trust. By being open and honest about your actions and intentions, you can demonstrate your commitment to recovery and rebuilding the relationship.

- Open Communication: Maintain open and honest communication with your loved ones. Share your progress in recovery, discuss challenges and setbacks, and be transparent about your actions and decisions. Open communication fosters trust and understanding.

- Regular Updates: Provide regular updates on your recovery journey. This can include sharing milestones, achievements, and any difficulties you encounter. Keeping your loved ones informed helps them feel involved and reassured about your commitment to change.

- Accountability: Be accountable for your actions by seeking feedback and support from your loved ones. Allow them to express their concerns and questions, and respond with honesty and transparency. Accountability demonstrates that you are taking responsibility for your recovery and the relationship.

4. Building Trust through Actions:

Rebuilding trust requires more than just words; it requires consistent actions that demonstrate your commitment to change.

- Avoiding Triggers: Take proactive steps to avoid triggers and high-risk situations that could lead to relapse. Show your loved ones that you are making conscious efforts to protect your recovery and the relationship.

- Seeking Professional Help: Engage in professional therapy or counseling to address the underlying issues of your gambling addiction. Demonstrating a commitment to professional help shows that you are serious about your recovery and willing to work on yourself.

- Involving Loved Ones: Involve your loved ones in your recovery journey. This can include attending therapy sessions together, participating in support groups, or seeking their input and support in your recovery plan. Involvement fosters a sense of partnership and collaboration.

5. Patience and Understanding:

Rebuilding trust is a gradual process that requires patience and understanding. Recognize that your loved ones may need time to heal and rebuild their trust in you.

- Respect Their Process: Respect the time and space your loved ones need to process their emotions and rebuild trust. Avoid pressuring them for immediate forgiveness or reconciliation. Trust takes time to rebuild, and their process should be honored.

- Demonstrate Empathy: Show empathy and understanding towards your loved ones' feelings and experiences. Acknowledge their pain and validate their emotions. Demonstrating empathy helps to rebuild emotional connections and foster a sense of understanding.

- Consistency Over Time: Consistently demonstrate positive change and reliability over time. Building trust is not a one-time effort but an ongoing commitment. Continue to show your loved ones that you are dedicated to maintaining a healthy and trustworthy relationship.

Effective Communication Strategies

EFFECTIVE COMMUNICATION is essential for rebuilding relationships and maintaining a healthy connection with loved ones. Here are strategies to improve communication and foster understanding.

1. Active Listening:

Active listening involves fully focusing on, understanding, and responding to your loved ones' messages. It shows that you value their perspective and are engaged in the conversation.

- Giving Full Attention: Give your full attention to the speaker by making eye contact, nodding, and using verbal affirmations like "I understand" or "Tell me more." Avoid distractions such as checking your phone or looking away.

- Reflecting and Paraphrasing: Reflect back what the speaker has said to ensure understanding. Use phrases like "What I hear you saying is..." or "It sounds like you feel..." to paraphrase their message. This demonstrates that you are actively listening and seeking to understand their perspective.

- Avoiding Interruptions: Allow the speaker to express their thoughts and feelings without interrupting. Resist the urge to formulate a response while they are speaking. Wait until they have finished before sharing your thoughts.

2. Expressing Emotions Clearly:

Expressing emotions clearly and constructively helps to communicate your feelings without causing conflict or misunderstanding.

- Using "I" Statements: Use "I" statements to express your feelings and needs. For example, say "I feel hurt when you do this" instead of "You always do this." This approach focuses on your emotions rather than placing blame on the other person.

- Describing Specific Behaviors: Be specific about the behaviors or actions that affect you. Instead of making generalizations like "You never listen to me," say "I feel ignored when you check your phone while I'm talking."

- Avoiding Accusations: Avoid making accusatory or judgmental statements that can escalate conflict. Focus on expressing your feelings and needs without attacking the other person.

3. Practicing Empathy:

Empathy involves understanding and sharing the feelings of another person. Practicing empathy helps to build emotional connections and foster a sense of understanding.

- Putting Yourself in Their Shoes: Try to see the situation from your loved one's perspective. Consider how they might be feeling and what they might be experiencing. This helps to build empathy and compassion.

- Validating Their Feelings: Acknowledge and validate your loved one's emotions, even if you don't fully understand or agree with them. Use phrases like "I can see why you feel that way" or "Your feelings are valid."

- Showing Support: Show support and understanding by offering comforting words or gestures. Let your loved one know that you are there for them and that you care about their well-being.

4. Managing Conflict Constructively:

Conflict is a natural part of any relationship, but managing it constructively is essential for maintaining a healthy connection.

- Staying Calm: Stay calm and composed during conflicts. Take deep breaths, count to ten, or take a short break if needed to regain your composure. Avoid raising your voice or using aggressive body language.

- Focusing on the Issue: Focus on the specific issue at hand rather than bringing up past grievances or unrelated problems. Addressing one issue at a time helps to keep the conversation productive and focused.

- Finding Common Ground: Look for areas of agreement and common ground. Acknowledge the points where you both agree and use them as a foundation for resolving the conflict.

- Seeking Solutions: Work together to find mutually acceptable solutions to the conflict. Be willing to compromise and consider each other's needs and perspectives.

5. Setting Boundaries:

Setting boundaries is essential for maintaining a healthy relationship and protecting your well-being.

- Identifying Boundaries: Identify your personal boundaries and communicate them clearly to your loved ones. Boundaries can include limits on time, emotional energy, and personal space.

- Communicating Boundaries: Communicate your boundaries respectfully and assertively. Use "I" statements to express your needs, such as "I need some time alone to recharge" or "I am not comfortable discussing this topic right now."

- Respecting Boundaries: Respect your loved ones' boundaries and encourage them to communicate their needs as well. Mutual respect for each other's boundaries helps to build trust and maintain a healthy relationship.

6. Engaging in Positive Communication:

Positive communication involves focusing on constructive and uplifting interactions that strengthen the relationship.

- Offering Praise and Appreciation: Offer praise and appreciation for your loved one's positive actions and qualities. Use specific examples to show your gratitude, such as "I appreciate how you always listen to me" or "Thank you for being supportive."

- Using Positive Language: Use positive and encouraging language in your interactions. Avoid negative or critical remarks that can damage the relationship.

- Engaging in Fun Activities: Engage in fun and enjoyable activities together to strengthen your bond. Shared experiences and positive interactions can enhance emotional connections and create lasting memories.

Participating in Family Therapy

FAMILY THERAPY INVOLVES working with a trained therapist to address issues within the family system and improve communication, understanding, and relationships. It can be particularly beneficial for families affected by gambling addiction.

1. Understanding Family Therapy:

Family therapy focuses on the dynamics and interactions within the family system. It aims to address the impact of gambling addiction on the family, improve communication, and promote healing.

- Goals of Family Therapy: The primary goals of family therapy are to improve communication, resolve conflicts, rebuild trust, and strengthen family bonds. It also aims to support the individual in recovery and address the needs of each family member.

- Types of Family Therapy: There are several types of family therapy, including structural family therapy, strategic family therapy, and systemic family therapy. Each approach has its unique techniques and focus areas, but all aim to improve family dynamics and relationships.

2. Benefits of Family Therapy:

Family therapy offers several benefits for families affected by gambling addiction.

- Improved Communication: Family therapy helps to improve communication within the family by teaching effective communication skills and fostering open and honest dialogue.

- Enhanced Understanding: Family therapy promotes understanding and empathy among family members. It helps each member understand the impact of gambling addiction and the challenges faced by the individual in recovery.

- Conflict Resolution: Family therapy provides tools and techniques for resolving conflicts constructively. It helps families address underlying issues and work towards mutually acceptable solutions.

- Rebuilding Trust: Family therapy supports the process of rebuilding trust by addressing the damage caused by gambling addiction and developing strategies for restoring stability and reliability.

- Supporting Recovery: Family therapy provides a supportive environment for the individual in recovery. It helps the family understand their role in supporting recovery and develop strategies to prevent relapse.

3. The Family Therapy Process:

The family therapy process typically involves several stages, including assessment, goal setting, intervention, and evaluation.

- Assessment: The therapist conducts an initial assessment to understand the family dynamics, identify issues, and gather information about each family member's perspective. This assessment helps to develop a tailored treatment plan.

- Goal Setting: The therapist works with the family to set specific and achievable goals for therapy. These goals may include improving communication, resolving conflicts, rebuilding trust, and supporting recovery.

- Intervention: The therapist uses various techniques and interventions to address the identified issues and work towards the therapy goals. This may include role-playing, communication exercises, and conflict resolution strategies.

- Evaluation: The therapist regularly evaluates progress and adjusts the treatment plan as needed. The evaluation helps to ensure that the therapy is effective and that the family is making progress towards their goals.

4. Techniques and Interventions in Family Therapy:

Family therapy involves various techniques and interventions to address issues and improve relationships.

- Communication Exercises: Communication exercises help family members practice effective communication skills, such as active listening, expressing emotions clearly, and managing conflict constructively.

- Role-Playing: Role-playing involves acting out scenarios to practice new behaviors and responses. It helps family members understand each other's perspectives and develop empathy.

- Genograms: Genograms are visual representations of the family tree that include information about relationships, conflicts, and patterns of behavior. They help to identify family dynamics and patterns that may contribute to issues.

- Problem-Solving Techniques: Problem-solving techniques involve identifying issues, generating solutions, and implementing action plans. These techniques help families address challenges constructively and work towards mutually acceptable solutions.

- Behavioral Contracts: Behavioral contracts are agreements between family members that outline specific behaviors and commitments. They help to set clear expectations and promote accountability.

5. Addressing Specific Issues in Family Therapy:

Family therapy can address various issues related to gambling addiction and its impact on the family.

- Financial Strain: Gambling addiction often leads to financial strain, which can cause stress and conflict within the family. Family therapy can help to develop strategies for managing finances, reducing debt, and restoring financial stability.

- Emotional Impact: The emotional impact of gambling addiction can affect all family members. Family therapy provides a space to process emotions, address trauma, and develop healthy coping mechanisms.

- Parenting Challenges: Gambling addiction can affect parenting and family dynamics. Family therapy can support parents in developing effective parenting strategies and fostering a positive family environment.

- Rebuilding Trust: Rebuilding trust is a central focus of family therapy. The therapist works with the family to develop strategies for restoring trust, such as consistent communication, accountability, and transparency.

6. Involving Children in Family Therapy:

Involving children in family therapy can be beneficial for addressing their needs and helping them understand the impact of gambling addiction.

- Age-Appropriate Communication: Use age-appropriate language and explanations when discussing gambling addiction and its impact. Help children understand the situation without overwhelming them with details.

- Creating a Safe Space: Ensure that therapy sessions provide a safe and supportive environment for children to express their feelings and concerns. Validate their emotions and provide reassurance.

- Supporting Emotional Well-Being: Address the emotional well-being of children by helping them develop healthy coping mechanisms and providing support for their emotional needs.

- Fostering Positive Relationships: Family therapy can help to strengthen the parent-child relationship and promote positive interactions. Encourage activities that foster bonding and connection.

7. Commitment to the Family Therapy Process:

Commitment to the family therapy process is essential for achieving positive outcomes. This involves active participation, openness to change, and a willingness to work together.

- Active Participation: Actively participate in therapy sessions by engaging in discussions, completing exercises, and practicing new skills. Active participation demonstrates a commitment to the therapy process and the family's well-being.

- Openness to Change: Be open to change and willing to try new approaches. Therapy often involves challenging existing patterns and behaviors, and openness to change is crucial for progress.

- Consistency: Attend therapy sessions consistently and follow through on commitments made during therapy. Consistency helps to build trust and demonstrate a commitment to positive change.

- Collaboration: Work collaboratively with the therapist and other family members. Collaboration fosters a sense of partnership and shared responsibility for the family's well-being.

Moving Forward

STRENGTHENING RELATIONSHIPS is a critical component of recovery from gambling addiction. Rebuilding trust with loved ones, effective communication strategies, and participating in family therapy are essential steps in this process.

Rebuilding trust with loved ones involves acknowledging the damage caused by gambling addiction, making amends, demonstrating consistency and transparency, building trust through actions, and practicing patience and understanding. These steps help to restore stability and reliability in relationships.

Effective communication strategies include active listening, expressing emotions clearly, practicing empathy, managing conflict constructively, setting boundaries, and engaging in positive communication. These strategies foster understanding, connection, and healthy interactions.

Participating in family therapy provides a structured and supportive environment for addressing issues within the family system. Family therapy helps to improve communication, resolve conflicts, rebuild trust, and support recovery. It involves various techniques and interventions tailored to the family's needs and goals.

As we continue to explore the various aspects of gambling addiction in this book, we will provide practical strategies and insights to support individuals and their families on their path to recovery. Understanding the importance of strengthening relationships is a crucial step in this process, as it equips individuals and their loved ones with the knowledge and tools needed to rebuild their lives and relationships.

Together, we can build a brighter future free from the destructive impact of compulsive gambling. Whether you are personally struggling with gambling addiction or supporting someone who is, know that help is available and recovery is possible. Let us take the next step forward on this journey towards healing and recovery, strengthening relationships, and building a supportive and loving family environment.

Chapter 14: Long-term Recovery and Maintenance

Long-term recovery from gambling addiction requires ongoing commitment, effort, and dedication. It involves setting long-term goals, continually seeking self-improvement and growth, and celebrating milestones and achievements. This chapter explores strategies for sustaining long-term recovery, maintaining progress, and living a fulfilling and balanced life.

Setting Long-term Goals

SETTING LONG-TERM GOALS is essential for maintaining motivation and direction in recovery. Long-term goals provide a roadmap for the future and help individuals focus on positive and meaningful aspirations.

1. Understanding the Importance of Long-term Goals:

Long-term goals are crucial for sustaining recovery and building a fulfilling life. They provide a sense of purpose, structure, and motivation.

- Purpose and Meaning: Long-term goals give a sense of purpose and meaning to life. They help individuals focus on positive aspirations and contribute to personal growth and fulfillment.

- Structure and Direction: Long-term goals provide structure and direction, helping individuals stay focused on their recovery journey. They offer a clear path to follow and milestones to work towards.

- Motivation and Commitment: Long-term goals motivate individuals to stay committed to their recovery. They provide a sense of accomplishment and reinforce positive behavior.

2. Setting SMART Goals:

SMART goals are Specific, Measurable, Achievable, Relevant, and Time-bound. These criteria ensure that goals are clear, realistic, and actionable.

- Specific: Goals should be specific and clearly defined. Avoid vague or general goals. For example, instead of setting a goal to "improve finances," set a specific goal to "save $500 in an emergency fund by the end of the year."

- Measurable: Goals should be measurable so that progress can be tracked. Define specific metrics or criteria for measuring success. For example, a measurable goal could be "attend three support group meetings each month."

- Achievable: Goals should be realistic and achievable given the individual's current situation and resources. Avoid setting goals that are too ambitious or unattainable. For example, instead of setting a goal to "completely eliminate debt in six months," set a more achievable goal to "reduce debt by $2,000 over the next year."

- Relevant: Goals should be relevant and aligned with the individual's values, priorities, and recovery journey. Ensure that the goals contribute to long-term recovery and personal growth.

- Time-bound: Goals should have a specific timeframe for completion. Define deadlines or target dates for achieving the goals. For example, a time-bound goal could be "complete a certification course by the end of the year."

3. Identifying Key Areas for Long-term Goals:

Long-term goals can encompass various areas of life, including financial stability, career development, personal growth, health and wellness, relationships, and leisure activities.

- Financial Stability: Goals related to financial stability may include saving money, reducing debt, creating a budget, or investing for the future. Financial stability provides a sense of security and reduces stress.

- Career Development: Goals related to career development may include advancing in your current job, pursuing further education or training, or changing careers. Career development provides a sense of achievement and purpose.

- Personal Growth: Goals related to personal growth may include learning new skills, pursuing hobbies and interests, or engaging in self-improvement activities. Personal growth contributes to overall well-being and fulfillment.

- Health and Wellness: Goals related to health and wellness may include regular exercise, healthy eating, regular medical check-ups, or practicing mindfulness and relaxation techniques. Health and wellness are essential for physical and mental well-being.

- Relationships: Goals related to relationships may include improving communication, rebuilding trust, spending quality time with loved ones, or expanding your social network. Healthy relationships provide support and connection.

- Leisure Activities: Goals related to leisure activities may include traveling, participating in recreational activities, or exploring new hobbies. Leisure activities provide enjoyment and relaxation.

4. Creating an Action Plan:

Creating an action plan involves breaking down long-term goals into smaller, manageable steps. This approach makes goals less overwhelming and provides a clear path to follow.

- Breaking Down Goals: Break down long-term goals into smaller, achievable steps. Define specific actions or tasks required to achieve each step. For example, if the goal is to save $500 in an emergency fund, break it down into monthly savings targets.

- Setting Milestones: Set milestones or checkpoints to track progress towards long-term goals. Milestones provide a sense of accomplishment and motivation. For example, set quarterly milestones for reducing debt or completing a certification course.

- Creating a Timeline: Create a timeline for achieving each step and milestone. Define specific deadlines or target dates for completion. A timeline provides structure and ensures that progress is consistent.

- Monitoring Progress: Regularly monitor and review progress towards long-term goals. Adjust the action plan as needed based on progress and changing circumstances. Monitoring progress helps to stay on track and make necessary adjustments.

5. Staying Committed to Long-term Goals:

Staying committed to long-term goals requires ongoing effort, motivation, and resilience. Here are strategies to maintain commitment and motivation.

- Maintaining Motivation: Find sources of motivation that inspire and drive you towards your goals. This can include visualizing the positive outcomes of achieving your goals, seeking support from loved ones, or rewarding yourself for progress.

- Overcoming Challenges: Anticipate and address potential challenges that may arise on the path to achieving your goals. Develop strategies for overcoming obstacles and staying focused on your goals.

- Seeking Support: Seek support from friends, family, support groups, or professionals to stay committed to your goals. Support provides encouragement, accountability, and guidance.

- Practicing Resilience: Practice resilience by staying positive, adaptable, and persistent. Recognize that setbacks are a normal part of the journey and use them as learning opportunities.

Continual Self-improvement and Growth

CONTINUAL SELF-IMPROVEMENT and growth are essential for sustaining long-term recovery and building a fulfilling life. This involves seeking opportunities for learning, personal development, and self-discovery.

1. Embracing Lifelong Learning:

Lifelong learning involves continuously seeking knowledge, skills, and experiences that contribute to personal and professional growth.

- Pursuing Education: Consider pursuing further education or training to enhance your skills and knowledge. This can include enrolling in courses, attending workshops, or pursuing certifications. Education opens up new opportunities and contributes to personal growth.

- Reading and Researching: Make reading and researching a regular habit. Explore books, articles, and online resources related to your interests, career, or personal development. Reading broadens your perspective and deepens your understanding.

- Learning New Skills: Continuously seek opportunities to learn new skills. This can include technical skills, creative skills, or practical skills. Learning new skills enhances your capabilities and boosts confidence.

2. Setting Personal Development Goals:

Personal development goals focus on improving various aspects of your life, including your mindset, habits, and behaviors.

- Improving Mindset: Set goals to develop a positive and growth-oriented mindset. This can include practicing gratitude, positive thinking, and self-compassion. A positive mindset enhances resilience and well-being.

- Developing Healthy Habits: Set goals to develop and maintain healthy habits. This can include regular exercise, healthy eating, mindfulness practices, and self-care routines. Healthy habits contribute to overall well-being and long-term recovery.

- Enhancing Emotional Intelligence: Set goals to enhance your emotional intelligence, which includes self-awareness, self-regulation, empathy, and social skills. Emotional intelligence improves relationships and personal growth.

3. Exploring Hobbies and Interests:

Exploring hobbies and interests provides enjoyment, relaxation, and a sense of fulfillment. Engaging in activities you are passionate about contributes to overall well-being.

- Trying New Activities: Be open to trying new activities and exploring new interests. This can include creative pursuits, sports, outdoor activities, or social events. Trying new activities expands your horizons and brings new experiences.

- Developing Talents: Focus on developing and honing your talents and strengths. Whether it's playing a musical instrument, painting, writing, or cooking, developing your talents brings a sense of accomplishment and joy.

- Participating in Groups or Clubs: Join groups or clubs related to your hobbies and interests. This provides opportunities for social interaction, learning, and shared experiences. Being part of a community fosters connection and support.

4. Fostering Personal Growth through Reflection:

Reflection is a powerful tool for personal growth and self-improvement. Regular reflection helps to evaluate your progress, understand your experiences, and identify areas for growth.

- Journaling: Maintain a journal to record your thoughts, feelings, experiences, and goals. Journaling provides a space for self-reflection and insight. Reflect on your achievements, challenges, and lessons learned.

- Self-assessment: Conduct regular self-assessments to evaluate your progress towards your goals and personal growth. Identify your strengths and areas for improvement. Self-assessment promotes self-awareness and continuous growth.

- Setting New Goals: Based on your reflections and self-assessments, set new goals for personal development and growth. Continuously seek opportunities for improvement and strive to become the best version of yourself.

5. Building a Supportive Environment:

A supportive environment is essential for continual self-improvement and growth. Surround yourself with individuals and resources that inspire and support your journey.

- Seeking Mentorship: Seek mentorship from individuals who have experience and expertise in areas you want to grow. Mentors provide guidance, support, and valuable insights.

- Connecting with Like-minded Individuals: Connect with like-minded individuals who share your interests and goals. Join communities, forums, or social groups that align with your passions and aspirations. Building connections fosters motivation and support.

- Creating a Positive Environment: Create a positive and supportive environment at home and work. Surround yourself with positivity, encouragement, and resources that promote growth and well-being.

Celebrating Milestones and Achievements

CELEBRATING MILESTONES and achievements is essential for maintaining motivation and recognizing progress in your recovery journey. It reinforces positive behavior, boosts confidence, and provides a sense of accomplishment.

1. Recognizing Milestones:

Milestones are significant markers of progress towards your long-term goals. Recognizing and celebrating milestones provides motivation and a sense of achievement.

- Identifying Milestones: Identify key milestones in your recovery journey and long-term goals. These can include achieving a specific period of sobriety, reaching a financial target, completing a course, or developing a new skill.

- Tracking Progress: Keep track of your progress towards milestones. Use journals, charts, or apps to monitor your achievements. Tracking progress helps you stay focused and motivated.

- Celebrating Milestones: Celebrate milestones in meaningful and enjoyable ways. This can include treating yourself to something special, spending time with loved ones, or engaging in activities that bring joy. Celebrating milestones reinforces positive behavior and provides a sense of accomplishment.

2. Acknowledging Achievements:

Acknowledging achievements involves recognizing and appreciating the progress you have made and the hard work you have put into your recovery and personal growth.

- Reflecting on Achievements: Take time to reflect on your achievements and the efforts that led to them. Recognize the challenges you have overcome and the skills and strengths you have developed.

- Expressing Gratitude: Express gratitude for the progress you have made and the support you have received. Gratitude fosters a positive mindset and enhances well-being.

- Sharing Achievements: Share your achievements with loved ones, support groups, or mentors. Sharing your successes provides encouragement and inspiration to others and reinforces your sense of accomplishment.

3. Rewarding Yourself:

Rewarding yourself for achievements and milestones provides motivation and reinforces positive behavior. Choose rewards that are meaningful and aligned with your values and goals.

- Meaningful Rewards: Choose rewards that are meaningful and contribute to your well-being and happiness. This can include experiences, activities, or items that bring joy and fulfillment.

- Healthy Rewards: Ensure that rewards are healthy and supportive of your recovery journey. Avoid rewards that may trigger relapse or unhealthy behavior. Focus on rewards that promote well-being and positive growth.

- Balanced Rewards: Balance rewards with your long-term goals and responsibilities. Ensure that rewards do not compromise your financial stability, health, or other important aspects of your life.

4. Reflecting on Growth and Progress:

Regularly reflecting on your growth and progress helps to recognize how far you have come and the positive changes you have made.

- Journaling: Use journaling as a tool for reflecting on your growth and progress. Write about your achievements, challenges, and lessons learned. Reflecting through journaling provides insight and perspective.

- Self-assessment: Conduct regular self-assessments to evaluate your progress and growth. Identify areas where you have made significant improvements and areas that need further development.

- Setting New Goals: Based on your reflections, set new goals for continued growth and improvement. Continuously seek opportunities for personal development and strive to achieve new milestones.

5. Fostering a Positive Mindset:

A positive mindset is essential for celebrating achievements and maintaining motivation. Focus on the positive aspects of your journey and the progress you have made.

- Practicing Gratitude: Practice gratitude by regularly reflecting on the positive aspects of your life and the progress you have made. Keep a gratitude journal and write about things you are grateful for each day.

- Positive Affirmations: Use positive affirmations to reinforce a positive mindset. Repeat affirmations that focus on your strengths, achievements, and potential. Positive affirmations boost confidence and motivation.

- Surrounding Yourself with Positivity: Surround yourself with positive influences and resources. This can include inspirational books, motivational quotes, supportive individuals, and uplifting environments. Positivity fosters resilience and well-being.

Moving Forward

LONG-TERM RECOVERY and maintenance require ongoing commitment, effort, and dedication. Setting long-term goals, continual self-improvement and growth, and celebrating milestones and achievements are essential for sustaining recovery and building a fulfilling life.

Setting long-term goals provides purpose, structure, and motivation. Goals should be specific, measurable, achievable, relevant, and time-bound (SMART). Identify key areas for long-term goals, create an action plan, and stay committed to achieving them.

Continual self-improvement and growth involve embracing lifelong learning, setting personal development goals, exploring hobbies and interests, fostering personal growth through reflection, and building a supportive environment. Continual growth contributes to overall well-being and fulfillment.

Celebrating milestones and achievements provides motivation, reinforces positive behavior, and boosts confidence. Recognize milestones, acknowledge achievements, reward yourself, reflect on growth and progress, and foster a positive mindset.

As we continue to explore the various aspects of gambling addiction in this book, we will provide practical strategies and insights to support individuals on their path to recovery. Understanding the importance of long-term recovery and maintenance is a crucial step in this process, as it equips individuals with the knowledge and tools needed to overcome addiction and build a fulfilling life.

Together, we can build a brighter future free from the destructive impact of compulsive gambling. Whether you are personally struggling with gambling addiction or supporting someone who is, know that help is available and recovery is possible. Let us take the next step forward on this journey towards healing and recovery, long-term growth, and a fulfilling life.

Chapter 15: Sharing Your Journey

Sharing your journey of recovery from gambling addiction can be a powerful and transformative experience. It not only helps inspire others who are facing similar challenges but also reinforces your commitment to recovery. By becoming a mentor or advocate, you can give back to the community and contribute to a larger movement of support and understanding. This chapter explores the benefits of sharing your story, how to become a mentor or advocate, and the importance of giving back.

Inspiring Others with Your Story

SHARING YOUR STORY of recovery can inspire others to seek help, make positive changes, and stay committed to their recovery journey. It can provide hope, encouragement, and a sense of connection to those who may feel isolated or hopeless.

1. Understanding the Impact of Your Story:

Your personal story of recovery has the potential to make a significant impact on others. It can resonate with those who are struggling with similar challenges and provide a sense of hope and possibility.

- Providing Hope: Sharing your journey can provide hope to those who are struggling with gambling addiction. Hearing about your successes and the obstacles you have overcome can inspire others to believe that recovery is possible.

- Encouraging Action: Your story can encourage others to take action towards their own recovery. It can motivate them to seek help, join support groups, or take the first step towards change.

- Creating Connection: Sharing your story can create a sense of connection and understanding. It helps others feel less alone and validates their experiences and emotions.

2. Preparing to Share Your Story:

Before sharing your story, it is important to reflect on your journey and consider the key messages you want to convey. Preparation helps to ensure that your story is impactful and resonates with your audience.

- Reflecting on Your Journey: Take time to reflect on your recovery journey. Consider the key milestones, challenges, and successes that have shaped your experience. Reflect on the lessons you have learned and the strategies that have helped you.

- Identifying Key Messages: Identify the key messages you want to convey in your story. This can include the importance of seeking help, the power of resilience, the benefits of support groups, or the value of self-care. Focus on messages that can inspire and motivate others.

- Structuring Your Story: Structure your story in a way that is clear and engaging. Consider using a chronological approach, starting with your struggles, moving on to your turning point, and concluding with your recovery and ongoing journey. Highlight key moments and turning points that have had a significant impact on your recovery.

3. Sharing Your Story in Different Settings:

There are various settings in which you can share your story, each with its unique opportunities and considerations.

- Support Groups: Sharing your story in support groups such as Gamblers Anonymous or SMART Recovery provides a safe and supportive environment. Your story can inspire and encourage fellow group members who are on a similar journey.

- Community Events: Participating in community events, such as addiction awareness campaigns or recovery fairs, allows you to reach a broader audience.

Your story can raise awareness about gambling addiction and the importance of seeking help.

- Online Platforms: Sharing your story on online platforms, such as blogs, social media, or recovery forums, can reach a wide and diverse audience. Online platforms provide an opportunity to connect with individuals who may not have access to in-person support.

- Public Speaking: Public speaking engagements, such as conferences, workshops, or educational seminars, allow you to share your story with larger audiences. Public speaking can amplify your message and inspire a broader community.

4. Overcoming Challenges in Sharing Your Story:

Sharing your personal story can be challenging, especially when it involves discussing difficult experiences and emotions. It is important to address these challenges and prepare for potential reactions.

- Managing Vulnerability: Sharing your story requires vulnerability and openness. It is normal to feel apprehensive about exposing personal experiences. Remind yourself of the positive impact your story can have and the support available to you.

- Handling Reactions: Be prepared for a range of reactions from your audience. Some individuals may respond with empathy and support, while others may have different perspectives. Stay focused on the positive impact of your story and the encouragement you can provide.

- Setting Boundaries: Set boundaries to protect your well-being. Decide what aspects of your story you are comfortable sharing and what you prefer to keep private. Respect your own limits and prioritize your emotional health.

5. The Benefits of Sharing Your Story:

Sharing your story can have numerous benefits for both you and your audience. It can reinforce your commitment to recovery and contribute to personal growth and healing.

- Reinforcing Commitment: Sharing your story reinforces your commitment to recovery. It serves as a reminder of the progress you have made and the positive changes in your life. Publicly sharing your journey can strengthen your resolve to maintain sobriety.

- Personal Growth: Sharing your story promotes self-reflection and personal growth. It encourages you to reflect on your experiences, recognize your strengths, and celebrate your achievements. This process contributes to ongoing self-improvement and resilience.

- Building Empathy and Connection: Sharing your story builds empathy and connection with others. It fosters a sense of community and support, helping others feel understood and validated. Building connections with individuals who share similar experiences can enhance your support network.

- Contributing to a Larger Movement: Sharing your story contributes to a larger movement of awareness and support for individuals affected by gambling addiction. Your story can help reduce stigma, raise awareness, and promote understanding within the community.

Becoming a Mentor or Advocate

BECOMING A MENTOR OR advocate allows you to use your experiences and knowledge to support others in their recovery journey. Mentorship and advocacy provide opportunities for personal growth, leadership, and community involvement.

1. Understanding the Role of a Mentor:

A mentor provides guidance, support, and encouragement to individuals who are navigating their recovery journey. Mentorship involves sharing experiences, offering advice, and being a positive role model.

- Providing Guidance: As a mentor, you provide guidance based on your own recovery experience. You offer practical advice, share strategies that have worked for you, and help mentees navigate challenges.

- Offering Support: Mentors offer emotional support and encouragement. You listen to your mentees, validate their experiences, and provide reassurance during difficult times.

- Being a Role Model: As a mentor, you serve as a positive role model for your mentees. Your commitment to recovery and positive changes in your life inspire and motivate others to stay committed to their journey.

2. Steps to Becoming a Mentor:

Becoming a mentor involves preparation, training, and a commitment to supporting others. Here are steps to becoming an effective mentor.

- Reflecting on Your Readiness: Reflect on your readiness to take on the role of a mentor. Ensure that you are in a stable and positive place in your recovery journey. Mentorship requires time, energy, and emotional resilience.

- Seeking Training: Seek training or workshops that provide mentorship skills and guidance. Many organizations offer mentorship training programs that cover topics such as communication, boundaries, and support strategies.

- Connecting with Support Groups: Connect with support groups or recovery organizations that offer mentorship programs. These organizations can provide opportunities to become a mentor and match you with mentees.

- Setting Boundaries: Set clear boundaries to protect your well-being and maintain a healthy mentor-mentee relationship. Define your availability, communication preferences, and limits on the level of support you can provide.

3. Mentorship in Action:

Effective mentorship involves ongoing support, regular communication, and a commitment to the mentee's growth and well-being.

- Regular Check-ins: Schedule regular check-ins with your mentee to discuss their progress, challenges, and goals. Regular communication provides consistent support and fosters a strong mentor-mentee relationship.

- Active Listening: Practice active listening to understand your mentee's experiences and needs. Show empathy, ask open-ended questions, and provide a safe space for them to express their thoughts and feelings.

- Setting Goals: Work with your mentee to set realistic and achievable goals for their recovery journey. Provide guidance on how to break down goals into manageable steps and celebrate their achievements along the way.

- Offering Resources: Share resources, such as books, articles, support groups, or workshops, that can support your mentee's recovery. Providing valuable resources helps them access additional support and information.

4. Understanding the Role of an Advocate:

An advocate raises awareness, promotes understanding, and supports policy changes related to gambling addiction and recovery. Advocacy involves speaking out on behalf of those affected by gambling addiction and working towards positive change.

- Raising Awareness: Advocates raise awareness about gambling addiction and its impact on individuals and communities. They share information, educate the public, and challenge misconceptions and stigma.

- Promoting Understanding: Advocacy promotes understanding and empathy towards individuals affected by gambling addiction. Advocates share personal stories, provide insights into the challenges of addiction, and encourage a compassionate response.

- Supporting Policy Changes: Advocates support policy changes that promote prevention, treatment, and support for gambling addiction. They work with organizations, policymakers, and community leaders to advocate for improved resources and services.

5. Steps to Becoming an Advocate:

Becoming an advocate involves education, collaboration, and a commitment to creating positive change. Here are steps to becoming an effective advocate.

- Educating Yourself: Educate yourself about gambling addiction, its impact, and the resources available for prevention and treatment. Stay informed about current research, policies, and best practices in the field.

- Joining Advocacy Organizations: Join advocacy organizations or coalitions that focus on gambling addiction and recovery. These organizations provide opportunities for advocacy, training, and collaboration.

- Building Relationships: Build relationships with other advocates, policymakers, community leaders, and organizations. Collaboration and networking are essential for effective advocacy.

- Sharing Your Story: Share your personal story as part of your advocacy efforts. Personal stories can have a powerful impact on raising awareness and promoting understanding.

6. ADVOCACY IN ACTION:

Effective advocacy involves various activities and initiatives that contribute to raising awareness, supporting policy changes, and promoting understanding.

- Public Speaking: Participate in public speaking engagements, such as conferences, workshops, or community events, to share your story and raise awareness about gambling addiction.

- Writing and Publishing: Write articles, blogs, or op-eds to share information and insights about gambling addiction. Publish your work in newspapers, magazines, online platforms, or organizational newsletters.

- Social Media Campaigns: Use social media to raise awareness and promote understanding. Share information, personal stories, and advocacy messages on platforms such as Facebook, Twitter, Instagram, or LinkedIn.

- Advocacy Campaigns: Participate in or organize advocacy campaigns to support policy changes and improve resources for gambling addiction.

Campaigns can include petition drives, letter-writing campaigns, or advocacy days at the legislature.

The Importance of Giving Back

GIVING BACK TO THE community and supporting others in their recovery journey is an essential aspect of long-term recovery. It provides a sense of purpose, reinforces positive behavior, and contributes to a larger movement of support and understanding.

1. The Benefits of Giving Back:

Giving back offers numerous benefits for both the giver and the recipient. It enhances personal growth, strengthens recovery, and fosters a sense of connection and community.

- Personal Growth: Giving back promotes personal growth by encouraging self-reflection, empathy, and compassion. It provides opportunities to develop new skills, build confidence, and enhance self-awareness.

- Strengthening Recovery: Giving back reinforces positive behavior and commitment to recovery. It serves as a reminder of the progress made and the positive impact of recovery. Helping others strengthens your resolve to maintain sobriety.

- Fostering Connection: Giving back fosters a sense of connection and community. It creates opportunities to build relationships, share experiences, and support others. Connection and community are essential for well-being and resilience.

2. Ways to Give Back:

There are various ways to give back and support others in their recovery journey. Choose activities that align with your interests, skills, and availability.

- Volunteering: Volunteer with organizations or support groups that focus on gambling addiction and recovery. Offer your time and skills to support their initiatives and activities.

- Mentorship: Become a mentor to individuals who are navigating their recovery journey. Provide guidance, support, and encouragement based on your own experiences.

- Advocacy: Participate in advocacy efforts to raise awareness, promote understanding, and support policy changes related to gambling addiction. Use your voice and experiences to advocate for positive change.

- Support Groups: Facilitate or participate in support groups for individuals affected by gambling addiction. Share your story, offer advice, and create a supportive environment for recovery.

- Community Involvement: Get involved in community initiatives that promote health, well-being, and recovery. Participate in events, campaigns, or workshops that support the recovery community.

3. Creating a Giving Back Plan:

Creating a giving back plan involves identifying opportunities to give back, setting goals, and committing to regular involvement.

- Identifying Opportunities: Identify opportunities to give back within your community or support networks. Consider volunteering, mentorship, advocacy, or participation in support groups. Choose activities that align with your interests and skills.

- Setting Goals: Set specific goals for your giving back activities. Define what you want to achieve and how you plan to contribute. For example, set a goal to volunteer a certain number of hours each month or to participate in a specific advocacy campaign.

- Committing to Regular Involvement: Commit to regular involvement in your chosen activities. Consistency is essential for making a meaningful impact and maintaining your commitment to giving back.

4. Reflecting on the Impact of Giving Back:

Regularly reflect on the impact of your giving back activities and the positive changes they have brought to your life and the lives of others.

- Personal Reflection: Reflect on how giving back has contributed to your personal growth and recovery. Consider the skills you have developed, the relationships you have built, and the sense of fulfillment you have gained.

- Feedback from Others: Seek feedback from the individuals or organizations you have supported. Understand the impact of your contributions and how they have made a difference in the lives of others.

- Adjusting Your Plan: Based on your reflections and feedback, adjust your giving back plan as needed. Explore new opportunities, set new goals, and continue to seek ways to make a positive impact.

Moving Forward

SHARING YOUR JOURNEY of recovery, becoming a mentor or advocate, and giving back to the community are powerful ways to reinforce your commitment to recovery and make a positive impact on others. These activities provide a sense of purpose, strengthen your resolve, and contribute to a larger movement of support and understanding.

Inspiring others with your story involves understanding the impact of your experiences, preparing to share your story, overcoming challenges, and recognizing the benefits of sharing. Your story can provide hope, encourage action, and create connections with others who are facing similar challenges.

Becoming a mentor or advocate involves providing guidance, support, and encouragement to individuals in their recovery journey. It includes seeking training, connecting with support groups, and engaging in advocacy activities to raise awareness and promote understanding.

The importance of giving back lies in the personal growth, strengthened recovery, and sense of connection it provides. There are various ways to give back, including volunteering, mentorship, advocacy, and community involvement. Creating a giving back plan and reflecting on the impact of your contributions ensures that your efforts are meaningful and impactful.

As we conclude this book, remember that recovery is a lifelong journey. By sharing your story, becoming a mentor or advocate, and giving back to the community, you can make a positive difference in the lives of others and contribute to a brighter future free from the destructive impact of compulsive gambling. Whether you are personally struggling with gambling addiction or supporting someone who is, know that help is available, and recovery is possible. Let us continue this journey towards healing, recovery, and a fulfilling life, together.

Conclusion

The journey of recovering from gambling addiction is challenging, but it is also a path filled with growth, learning, and transformation. Throughout this book, we have explored various aspects of gambling addiction, from understanding the underlying causes to developing strategies for long-term recovery. This conclusion will recap the key points covered in the book, offer encouragement and motivation for ongoing recovery, and provide resources for further support.

Recap of Key Points

THIS BOOK HAS PROVIDED a comprehensive guide to understanding and overcoming gambling addiction. Here is a recap of the key points covered in each chapter:

Chapter 1: Understanding Compulsive Gambling

- Defined gambling addiction and its types.

- Explored psychological and physiological factors contributing to gambling addiction.

- Discussed how gambling affects the brain and behavior.

Chapter 2: Recognizing the Signs

- Identified early warning signs of gambling addiction.

- Discussed behavioral, emotional, and physical indicators.

- Provided self-assessment tools to evaluate gambling behavior.

Chapter 3: The Impact of Gambling Addiction

- Examined the financial consequences of gambling addiction.

- Analyzed the effects on relationships and family life.

- Explored the mental and physical health repercussions of gambling addiction.

Chapter 4: The Psychology Behind Gambling

- Discussed the thrill of risk-taking and its appeal in gambling.

- Explored the role of escapism and stress relief in gambling behavior.

- Explained the gambling cycle and its impact on addiction.

Chapter 5: Breaking the Denial

- Addressed the importance of overcoming shame and guilt.

- Emphasized the need to accept the problem and seek help.

- Highlighted the role of self-awareness in breaking denial.

Chapter 6: Building a Support System

- Discussed the importance of involving family and friends in recovery.

- Explored support groups and therapy options.

- Provided strategies for creating a safe and understanding environment.

Chapter 7: Financial Recovery and Management

- Outlined steps for assessing financial damage caused by gambling.

- Discussed developing a financial recovery plan and budgeting wisely.

- Emphasized the importance of building an emergency fund and reducing debt.

Chapter 8: Developing Healthy Habits

- Explored ways to replace gambling with positive activities.

- Discussed building new hobbies and interests.

- Emphasized the importance of focusing on physical and mental well-being.

Chapter 9: Mindfulness and Stress Management

- Provided techniques for reducing stress and anxiety.

- Discussed the practice of mindfulness and meditation.

- Highlighted the benefits of maintaining a balanced lifestyle.

Chapter 10: Overcoming Triggers and Urges

- Identified strategies for recognizing and avoiding triggers.

- Explored coping mechanisms for managing cravings.

- Emphasized the importance of staying committed to recovery.

Chapter 11: Therapy and Counseling Options

- Discussed the benefits of cognitive-behavioral therapy (CBT).

- Explored the role of group therapy and peer support.

- Examined other therapeutic approaches for treating gambling addiction.

Chapter 12: Relapse Prevention

- Explained the nature of relapse and its role in recovery.

- Provided strategies for maintaining progress and preventing relapse.

- Offered guidance on what to do if a relapse occurs.

Chapter 13: Strengthening Relationships

- Addressed the importance of rebuilding trust with loved ones.

- Provided effective communication strategies.

- Discussed the benefits of participating in family therapy.

Chapter 14: Long-term Recovery and Maintenance

- Emphasized the importance of setting long-term goals.

- Discussed continual self-improvement and growth.

- Highlighted the importance of celebrating milestones and achievements.

Chapter 15: Sharing Your Journey

- Encouraged inspiring others by sharing your recovery story.

- Discussed becoming a mentor or advocate.

- Emphasized the importance of giving back to the community.

Encouragement and Motivation for Ongoing Recovery

RECOVERY FROM GAMBLING addiction is a lifelong journey that requires ongoing commitment, effort, and dedication. Here are some words of encouragement and motivation to support you on this path:

1. Embrace the Journey:

Recovery is not a destination but a continuous journey of growth and self-discovery. Embrace each step of the process, recognizing that every effort you make contributes to your well-being and future. Celebrate your progress, no matter how small, and keep moving forward with determination and resilience.

2. Stay Committed:

Commitment is the cornerstone of recovery. Stay focused on your goals and remind yourself of the reasons why you chose to embark on this journey. Whether it's to improve your health, rebuild relationships, achieve financial stability, or find personal fulfillment, keep these motivations at the forefront of your mind.

3. Seek Support:

You are not alone in your recovery journey. Seek support from loved ones, support groups, therapists, and mentors. Surround yourself with individuals who understand your struggles and can offer encouragement, guidance, and accountability. Building a strong support network can provide the strength and motivation you need to stay committed.

4. Practice Self-compassion:

Be kind and compassionate to yourself. Recovery is challenging, and setbacks are a normal part of the process. Instead of being critical of yourself, practice self-compassion. Acknowledge your efforts, recognize your strengths, and forgive yourself for any mistakes. Treat yourself with the same kindness and understanding that you would offer to a friend.

5. Focus on Progress, Not Perfection:

Recovery is not about achieving perfection but about making consistent progress. Focus on the positive changes you have made and the steps you are taking towards a healthier and more fulfilling life. Celebrate your achievements and learn from any setbacks. Progress, no matter how small, is a sign of growth and resilience.

6. Stay Positive and Hopeful:

Maintain a positive and hopeful outlook on your recovery journey. Believe in your ability to overcome challenges and achieve your goals. Stay motivated by visualizing the positive outcomes of your efforts and the life you want to create. Hope and positivity can fuel your determination and inspire you to keep moving forward.

7. Take Care of Your Well-being:

Prioritize your physical, mental, and emotional well-being. Engage in activities that promote relaxation, joy, and fulfillment. Practice mindfulness, exercise regularly, eat a balanced diet, and get enough sleep. Taking care of your well-being enhances your resilience and supports your recovery.

8. Embrace Personal Growth:

View recovery as an opportunity for personal growth and self-improvement. Seek opportunities to learn, develop new skills, and explore new interests. Embrace the changes and challenges as opportunities for growth and self-discovery. Personal growth contributes to a fulfilling and meaningful life.

9. Give Back and Inspire Others:

Share your journey and inspire others who are facing similar challenges. Becoming a mentor or advocate allows you to give back to the community and support others in their recovery. Your story can provide hope, encouragement, and a sense of connection. Giving back reinforces your commitment to recovery and contributes to a larger movement of support and understanding.

Resources for Further Support

RECOVERY FROM GAMBLING addiction is a journey that requires ongoing support and resources. Here are some valuable resources to help you continue your recovery journey:

1. Support Groups:

Support groups provide a sense of community, shared understanding, and mutual support. Joining a support group can offer encouragement, accountability, and practical advice from individuals who have experienced similar challenges.

- Gamblers Anonymous (GA): Gamblers Anonymous is a 12-step support group for individuals recovering from gambling addiction. Meetings are held regularly in various locations, and online meetings are also available.

- SMART Recovery: SMART Recovery (Self-Management and Recovery Training) is a science-based support group that focuses on self-empowerment and self-reliance. Meetings are held in-person and online.

2. Therapy and Counseling:

Professional therapy and counseling provide valuable guidance, support, and strategies for overcoming gambling addiction and maintaining recovery.

- National Helpline for Problem Gambling: The National Helpline for Problem Gambling (1-800-522-4700) offers confidential support, information, and referrals to local resources.

- Therapists and Counselors: Seek therapists or counselors who specialize in addiction recovery. Many offer individual therapy, group therapy, and family therapy.

3. Financial Counseling:

Financial counseling can help you develop a plan to manage debt, rebuild financial stability, and achieve long-term financial goals.

- National Foundation for Credit Counseling (NFCC): The NFCC offers financial counseling services, including budgeting, debt management, and financial education.

- Financial Planners: Consider working with a certified financial planner who can provide personalized financial advice and support.

4. Educational Resources:

Educational resources provide information, tools, and strategies to support your recovery journey and personal growth.

- Books and Articles: Explore books and articles on gambling addiction, recovery strategies, mindfulness, and personal development. Some recommended books include "The Easy Way to Stop Gambling" by Allen Carr and "Overcoming Problem Gambling: A Guide for Problem and Compulsive Gamblers" by Alex Blaszczynski.

- Online Resources: Access online resources, such as recovery websites, forums, and educational platforms. Websites like the National Council on Problem Gambling (NCPG) and the International Centre for Responsible Gambling (ICRG) offer valuable information and support.

5. Advocacy and Volunteer Organizations:

Getting involved in advocacy and volunteer organizations allows you to give back, raise awareness, and support others in their recovery journey.

- Advocacy Groups: Join advocacy groups that focus on gambling addiction and recovery. These organizations work to raise awareness, promote understanding, and support policy changes.

- Volunteer Opportunities: Volunteer with organizations that provide support and resources for individuals affected by gambling addiction. Volunteering allows you to make a positive impact and contribute to the community.

6. Mindfulness and Well-being Apps:

Mindfulness and well-being apps provide tools and resources to support your mental and emotional well-being.

- Headspace: Headspace offers guided meditation and mindfulness exercises to help reduce stress and improve mental well-being.

- Calm: Calm provides relaxation techniques, sleep stories, and meditation exercises to support overall well-being.

- MyFitnessPal: MyFitnessPal helps you track your nutrition and exercise, promoting a healthy lifestyle and physical well-being.

7. Online Support Communities:

Online support communities provide a platform to connect with others, share experiences, and seek advice and encouragement.

- Reddit: Subreddits like r/problemgambling and r/stopgambling offer a supportive community for individuals recovering from gambling addiction.

- Forums: Join forums and online communities dedicated to recovery and personal growth. These platforms provide a space to share experiences, seek support, and connect with others.

Moving Forward

AS WE CONCLUDE THIS book, remember that recovery from gambling addiction is a lifelong journey that requires ongoing effort, commitment, and dedication. The insights, strategies, and resources provided in this book are designed to support you on this path and empower you to build a fulfilling and meaningful life.

Recovery is not a linear process, and setbacks are a normal part of the journey. Embrace each step, celebrate your progress, and learn from your experiences. Stay committed to your goals, seek support from loved ones and professionals, and practice self-compassion and resilience.

Sharing your journey, becoming a mentor or advocate, and giving back to the community are powerful ways to reinforce your commitment to recovery and make a positive impact on others. Your story can provide hope, encouragement, and inspiration to those facing similar challenges.

Whether you are personally struggling with gambling addiction or supporting someone who is, know that help is available, and recovery is possible. Together, we can build a brighter future free from the destructive impact of compulsive gambling. Let us continue this journey towards healing, recovery, and a fulfilling life, together.

Don't miss out!

Visit the website below and you can sign up to receive emails whenever Timothy Scott Phillips publishes a new book. There's no charge and no obligation.

https://books2read.com/r/B-A-KCQWC-HFEJF

BOOKS 2 READ

Connecting independent readers to independent writers.

About the Author

Timothy Scott Phillips is a dedicated author specializing in non-fiction self-help books that empower readers to overcome challenges and embrace personal growth. With a passion for mental health, resilience, and self-improvement, Timothy combines research-based insights with practical strategies to inspire lasting change. His work reflects a deep commitment to helping individuals navigate life's complexities, build confidence, and unlock their full potential. When he's not writing, Timothy enjoys mentoring, exploring nature, and connecting with his readers to share stories of transformation and hope. His books are a testament to the power of perseverance and the human spirit.

www.ingramcontent.com/pod-product-compliance
Lightning Source LLC
Chambersburg PA
CBHW021203130726

47988CB00002B/488